HOW TO MAKE MONEY OUT OF ANTIQUES

Judith Miller is co-founder of Miller's Publications, which created the best-selling *Miller's Price Guides*, including the *Miller's Antiques Price Guide*, which sells over 135,000 copies a year. She has written several highly successful books on antiques, interior design and period decorating, including *Period Details*, *Period Style*, *Victorian Style*, *Country Style* and *Period Finishes and Effects*. She makes regular appearances on TV and radio and lives in north London.

Gray Jolliffe is a highly successful cartoonist who has written and illustrated many books, including the *Wicked Willie* series, in conjunction with Peter Mayle. Other books include *Christmas Already Again*, *How to be a Happy Cat*, *The Unadulterated Cat*, *Girl Chasing* and *A Marriage Survival Guide*.

HOW TO MAKE
MONEY
OUT OF
ANTIQUES

My God – that's a Louis Quinze armoire... Talk about luck!

JUDITH MILLER

WITH CARTOONS BY GRAY JOLLIFFE

HOW TO MAKE MONEY OUT OF ANTIQUES

by **Judith Miller**

with cartoons by **Gray Jolliffe**

First published in Great Britain in 1995 by Miller's,
a division of Mitchell Beazley, both imprints of
Octopus Publishing Group Ltd,
2–4 Heron Quays,
London E14 4JP

Chief Contributor **John Wainwright**

Editor **Francesca Collin**

Designer **Emma Jones**

Art Director **Jacqui Small**

Executive Editor **Alison Starling**

Executive Art Editor **Larraine Shamwana**

Production **Heather O'Connell**

Index **Hilary Bird**

Illustrations by Karen Cochrane, John Hutchinson and Hard Lines, Oxford, England

Copyright © Octopus Publishing Group Ltd 1995
Reprinted 1997 (twice), 1998, 2000 (twice)

ISBN 1 85732 584 2

A CIP catalogue record for this book is available from the British Library

Miller's is a registered trademark of Octopus Publishing Group Ltd
Set in 9.5pt Garamond Book, 11pt Fenice Regular and 16pt Fenice Bold Ultra
Printed by Mackays of Chatham plc, Chatham, Kent

CONTENTS

Foreword   6

Introduction   8

Chapter One   14
THE ANTIQUES TRADE

Chapter Two   26
LEARNING ABOUT ANTIQUES

Chapter Three   34
WHAT TO LOOK FOR

Chapter Four   88
HOW TO BUY

Chapter Five   110
CLEANING, REPAIR AND RESTORATION

Chapter Six   132
HOW TO SELL

Chapter Seven   150
SETTING UP IN BUSINESS

Appendix   162
Tradespeak
Further Reading
Useful Addresses
Antiques Inventory

Index   172

FOREWORD

— £ —

As an impoverished student living in a run-down part of Edinburgh during the late 1960s, I bought a few cheap, old and rather pretty plates from one of the local junk shops that I passed every day on my way to and from the university. To me they simply provided a far more attractive and unusual means of decorating the walls of my room than posters. After a while, however, I became increasingly intrigued as to when and where the plates had been made, and who had made them. Later still, I became interested in their value.

Unfortunately my first foray into the world of antiques did not realize any profit to speak of. However, my original purchases gave me a tremendous amount of pleasure and, more significantly, whetted my appetite to the extent that for over 25 years now much of my life has revolved around researching, collecting, buying and selling antiques.

During this period the antiques trade has expanded enormously, much of it a direct response to ever-increasing public interest. Publications such as Miller's Price Guides and Miller's Antiques Checklists and television programmes like the BBC's Antiques Roadshow, which regularly boasts viewing figures as high as those of the most popular 'soaps', have fuelled demand and awareness to the point where items found in the attic now often reappear for sale at boot fairs or at auctions. The opportunities for the trade and public alike to make money out of antiques has risen correspondingly and the popularization of antiques has resulted not only in a greater number of buyers looking for genuine pieces, thereby pushing up prices, but also a considerable diversification and broadening of fields that are now generally considered as collectable or valuable.

Whether you want to become a full-time antique dealer, an enthusiastic collector, or you simply want to make some money on the side, to show a profit on antiques not only do you have to be able to predict what will become more valuable in the future, but also to know what is valuable now. More specifically, you need to know what to look for, where to buy it, where and how to sell it, and how much to sell it for.

The experience I have built up in these areas over the last 25 years has stood me in good stead. Having learnt from some early mistakes, I have invariably bought for a good price and sold (when I wanted to) for a better one (often much better). In the following pages I hope to pass on my knowledge to you. I also hope that subsequently you have as much fun and enjoyment out of buying, owning and selling antiques as I have.

JUDITH MILLER

INTRODUCTION

———— £ ————

Some 20 years ago I was looking for a coffee table to go in the sitting room of a house we had just moved to, and spotted something I thought might be suitable in the window of a junk shop in Midhurst, Sussex. It was a large and rather ugly wooden chest on a short, bulbous stand. I reckoned the lid of the chest would make the perfect top for my coffee table if it was removed and re-secured to the stand underneath. I paid £2 for the piece, although I might have beaten the dealer down to £1.50! Anyway, it turned out to be quite a good buy: the box section was used by the children for storing toys (until it disappeared during another house move some time later), and the lid-on-stand proved to be very functional, even if it did become increasingly less attractive as sections of its marquetry decoration were gradually lost through everyday wear and tear.

A few years later, however, a German antique dealer called round to see us. Just as I was about to put down on the table the steaming hot cup of coffee I had made him, he let out a muffled scream and grabbed my arm. Slightly stunned, I asked him whatever was the matter? 'I don't suppose you have the chest section of this piece?', he replied. 'We did', I said, 'but it's long gone.' 'Oh that's tragic', he moaned, 'this is (was) a very rare, early German piece. In good condition it would have fetched many thousands of pounds at auction.'

As joint author and publisher of *Miller's Antiques Price Guide,* this was embarrassing, to say the least. However, I like to think we all learn from our mistakes, and for me it was a salutary reminder of something I thought I'd learnt a long time before: if you don't want to miss out on making money out of antiques you have to become as knowledgeable as you possibly

8

can about the subject, develop a sense, or an 'eye', for spotting something that might be valuable, and if you're not sure about it find someone who is.

There are numerous examples of people owning valuable pieces and having no idea of their true worth. Some have a happy ending, like the story of the lady who for many years used, in blissful ignorance, a late-Ming blue and white bowl (from the Wanli Emperor period – 1573-1620) as her dog's water bowl. After some advice from a rather horrified new neighbour she put it into auction, where it fetched, in 1984, £5,000. More recently, in 1991, a couple rediscovered four salt cellars wrapped in an old newspaper and long-forgotten at the back of a wardrobe. Having taken them to the BBC's *Antiques Roadshow*, in Salisbury for valuation, they were astounded to learn that the cellars were silver-gilt and made in 1811-13 by Paul Storr for Rundell, Bridge & Rundell – soon after they made £66,000 at Sotheby's. Other examples have resulted in a not-so-fortunate outcome, at least for the original owner: a couple who recently moved house could not believe their luck when they discovered the vendor had left, among other 'rubbish', an unframed watercolour in the garage. Identified as *The River Hudson from Fort Puttnam*, by Washington F. Friend (c.1820-86), the painting sold at auction for £1,800.

Whether you just want to cash-in on items you already have in your house, you simply wish to furnish a new home, start collecting for pleasure or investment, or whether you intend to buy and sell antiques for a full- or part-time living, knowing what something is and what it's worth gives you the financial edge over any other interested parties – at the very least it will ensure that you are not ripped off. Consequently, Chapter Two (see pages 26-33) is designed to get you off on the right track by describing the best ways of researching and becoming knowledgeable about antiques and collectables.

The tremendous variety of objects considered both antique and collectable today means that it is nigh-on impossible to become an expert about all of them. It is highly unlikely, for example, that you will have either the time or the inclination to become very knowledgeable about subjects as diverse as Georgian furniture, Oriental ceramics, Roman glass, Art Deco jewelry and pop memorabilia, to name but a few. Moreover, it doesn't make much commercial sense: most successful dealers tend to be pretty knowledgeable about antiques in general, but specialize in one or two areas. Broadly speaking, this is the approach I would recommend.

In other words, learn the basics of what to look for with as many antiques and collectables as you have time for. Then, when you've discovered a few areas that really interest you – in my case it happened to be Oriental blue and white porcelain – find out as much as you can, to the point where you really can consider yourself an expert on the subject.

In a book of this size it is obviously impossible to cover every different type and make of antique and collectable in minute detail; there are numerous specialist titles available on virtually all of them, and there is a list of those that I feel are particularly useful at the end of the book. However, Chapter Three (see pages 34-87) covers all the major categories, listing the basic guidelines to what you should be looking for, what is worth buying, and what you should leave well alone.

Chapter Four (see pages 88-109) describes where and how to buy antiques and collectables. There are numerous outlets open to you, including: boot fairs; charity stalls; newspaper advertisements; junk shops; market stalls; local and international antiques fairs; auctions; antiques shops; dealers (various types), and collectors.

Bargains can be had from most of them, provided you know not only what you are buying, but also the appropriate way to buy - which can be quite different in each case. For example, haggling with certain types of market traders is not only sensible, it is often expected. Trying to hustle an exclusive Bond Street dealer is, on the other hand, not only inappropriate, and therefore a waste of time, but also might well result in you being shown the door. Similarly, knowing how and when to buy at auction - an activity that many newcomers feel, understandably, though unnecessarily, intimidated by - requires a very specific approach, which includes a thorough understanding of the various procedures involved and, as you will see, a large dose of self-discipline.

Whether you have owned a particular piece for a long time, or you've just bought it, you may have to decide if it needs repairing or restoring to improve not only its condition but also its worth. This is an area full of both opportunities and dangers. Thus, Chapter Five (see pages 110-131) covers the types of restoration to be left to a professional restorer, together with those that an amateur can tackle with confidence - knowing he or she will be making the item more saleable and valuable. There are far too many incidents, particularly with items of furniture, of enthusiastic but clumsy amateurs 'improving' a piece, only to discover when they come to sell it that they've made a costly mistake, and would have done far better to pass it on unrestored.

Well, you've found a valuable heirloom in the attic, or you've bought something for a good price (or better still, a 'steal'), and you may or may not have improved it a bit. How do you go about selling it in a way that will maximize your profit? Chapter Six (see pages 132-149) describes, as with buying antiques and collectables, the different opportunities available to you.

Areas covered include: via market stalls, antiques fairs and antiques shops; and to collectors and various types of dealer.

The outlet you choose to sell through will, to a large extent, depend on how much time you have available. If buying and selling antiques is a part-time hobby, selling at auction, taking an occasional stall at a local antiques fair, cultivating a friendly dealer, or contacting collectors, may be your best options. If, on the other hand, you want to become a full-time dealer, you must consider additional alternatives, such as establishing connections with a network of fellow antique dealers or taking on the commitment of a shop yourself and then tempting the general public inside.

With the exception of auctions where someone is selling on your behalf, all outlets demand different types of selling techniques. With some you have to hustle: the difference between the buying and selling price of a piece is, after taking into account all the various overheads, someone's profit (or loss). You have to make sure most, if not all, of that profit is yours. With other outlets, anything that even smacks of a 'hard sell' can be the kiss of death: you have to learn the difference between selling somebody something and helping them to buy, especially if you want to do business with them again.

If you are to make antiques your full-time living you have to put your business on a proper footing. It's no good trading for two or three years and thinking the tax man won't catch up with you – he will. Consequently, Chapter Seven (see pages 150-161) covers everything you need to know, including bookkeeping, accountancy and, if your business really starts to take off, V.A.T. (for which Customs and Excise offer special schemes to antique dealers). There is also information on insuring your antiques – something everyone who owns them should know about – including the steps you should take that will ensure you are compensated in full if the worse comes to the worst. Right at the back of the book you'll find some suggestions for further reading, useful addresses and a glossary of commonly used terms (Tradespeak) – after all, you will have to be able to speak the language if you want to be able to compete on an equal footing with the rest of the antiques trade.

However, Chapter One (see pages 14-25) begins with something equally important: a description of the antiques trade in general, who's who in it, how everybody relates to each other, and how pieces usually change hands within it – essential reading if you want to know how to make money out of antiques.

CHAPTER ONE

THE ANTIQUES TRADE

———————— £ ————————

If you intend to buy or sell antiques and collectables, you should have a clear understanding of how the antiques trade works. Most people would be surprised to learn that in boom times over fifty per cent of sales can take place within the trade – dealer to dealer. Indeed, it has been observed that if there were three antique dealers stranded alone on a desert island and a Chippendale chair was washed ashore, each of them would make a profit on it. This is not far from the truth. In an expanding market 'insider dealing' makes financial sense: dealers are desperate for new stock to sell to their clients and, of course, one of the more easily accessible sources of supply are their fellow traders.

Moreover, some dealers have access to certain clients, such as private collectors, that others do not have. If you are in the latter category, it is better to sell something on to someone who can shift it quickly, rather than have it sitting around for months on end, awaiting a suitable buyer or auction sale and taking up valuable space in storage or a shop. The cash the sale releases can then be used to purchase new stock (which is, of course, rising in price during a boom). That can be sold on again, and so it goes on.

A similar logic operates during times of recession: moving stock on within the trade means money isn't tied up for too long in unsold items, and thus helps everyone out with their cash-flow. As most dealers are under-capitalized, good cash-flow is vital if they are to service their borrowings, maintain their standard of living and stay in the antiques business.

It is important to point out that 'insider dealing' is a very different activity to the one perpetrated from time to time on the Stock Exchange, and is perfectly legal. However, it would not take place at all if there wasn't some profit in it for the seller each time a sale was made. This means, inevitably, that by the time the piece in question reaches the end of the dealers' buying and selling chain, and is bought by a member of the public, it costs a lot more than it did at the outset.

To understand how the chain works in practice, you first need to know who the main players are. In some respects the antiques dealer network is as complex as the Indian caste system. At the top of the pile are the dealers who own large, exclusive shops mainly located in London's West End. Their stock consists of a wide range of high-quality, traditional art and antiques, is tastefully displayed throughout a series of expensively decorated, inter-connecting rooms, and its value, at any one time, runs into millions of pounds.

Such dealers employ a large staff, usually consisting of four or five well-spoken, knowledgeable young men or women to help clients make their purchases, and a team of restorers behind the scenes, each one specializing in a different area – furniture, ceramics, silverware, paintings, etc. In addition, they run their own vans to pick up and deliver all round the country. If you also take into account West End leases and rents, which are invariably exorbitant, overseas travelling expenses, a large advertising budget, accountancy fees and other hidden costs, it is no wonder that the mark-up on their prices (which are never displayed, and available only on request) is over one hundred per cent – it has to be, or bankruptcy would ensue.

The main reason why these top West End dealers prosper is because of the type of client they attract. On the one hand they have long-standing connections with some of the wealthiest families and individuals in the country (and abroad), which

gives them access to some of the best pieces when their owners wish to sell them. On the other hand, many of their clients,
particularly those from the Middle East, will spend millions of
pounds a year on furnishing new homes or building up collections. Consequently, for the ordinary man in the street the old
maxim applies: 'if you have to ask the price, you can't afford it'.
Indeed, if you don't look as if your bank balance could take the
strain, you would probably be lucky to get past the receptionist
on the front door.

The second tier of the antique dealers' network is largely
London-based, although there are other 'members' dotted
around the country in the more affluent cities and towns.
While their shops are not the size of the emporiums owned by
dealers in the top tier, they are large and also in smart
locations: in London this means Knightsbridge, Kensington,
Chelsea and parts of the West End. A closely knit group, all are
members of B.A.D.A. (the British Antique Dealers Association).
Invariably honest, very knowledgeable in their chosen fields,
and strictly conservative in outlook – anything made after 1830
can not be considered an antique – they specialize in areas,
such as Georgian furniture, English porcelain, 17th- and 18th-
century silver and glass, and other *objets de vertu*. In other
words, the sort of good-quality stock that is always desirable
(here and overseas), and can therefore be relied upon to
provide a reasonably quick turnover. They obtain much of this
stock from the leading London auction rooms, and in so doing
have a major influence on current price levels.

The third tier of dealers are, at least in terms of location,
harder to pin down. They specialize in one area of interest and
can be found trading from outlets as diverse as a stall in an
'exclusive' antiques market, a Volvo estate car, a suitcase or
even via the telephone at home. To achieve success in their
chosen field – typical subjects include anything from Russian

icons, European treen, Oriental carpets, medieval tapestries, English silverware, Art Deco jewelry, etc. – specialist dealers rely on their expertise and reputation to establish a national or international network of clients and fellow dealers. The latter supply them with most, if not all, of their stock, while the former, their clients, are usually contacted direct by telephone; over-the-counter sales often become less important the more successful the specialist dealer is. It takes many years of hard work to build up these dealer-client networks, and can be expensive. For example, some of the top specialist dealers will attempt to attract new collectors and clients to their network by putting on exhibitions of their wares, backed up with costly, although discreet, advertising and elaborate catalogues.

However, while such specialist dealing is not always the most lucrative part of the antiques trade, it is certainly one of the most interesting, and the dealers who operate within it tend to be highly respected not only by their fellow dealers, but also by collectors (they are often collectors themselves), museum curators and academics in the field.

The fourth tier in the network is made up of an idiosyncratic group of dealers, who in many ways are as much in the business of selling interior design and decorating as they are antiques. They always have smart shops in smart locations, and the antiques on display are augmented with a wide range of soft furnishings, fabric and wallpaper samples. The top dealers in this bracket usually have good-quality antiques and works of art for sale, often at reasonable prices. Others, have a tendency to sell various pieces that have been 'adapted' for something other than their original purpose. For example, it's not unusual to find 18th- or 19th-century wine coolers with their tops removed and containing exotic plants, or Indian wooden carvings augmented with sheets of glass to make coffee tables, or overmantel mirrors as bedheads. Because they are arbiters of taste for a sizeable section of the population, these dealers can have a profound influence on what is and what isn't considered fashionable in antiques. Consequently, they can also have a powerful effect on market prices, particularly at auction.

The next group is made up of private dealers, who, in any hierarchical structure within the trade, are rather hard to place. At one end of the spectrum there might be a retired individual who buys various pieces at auction from time to time and, when he or she decides on keeping them no longer, sells them on to friends. Above that are the dealers who operate from home, perhaps topping-up a spouse's income or enjoying a second career now that the children have grown up. Often specializing in a specific area, such as fine art or ceramics, they buy to sell on to their clients, who will include top London dealers or overseas collectors. At the other end of the spectrum is the man or woman with a retail outlet in London's West End, who supplies millions of pounds worth of antiques, such as medieval tapestries or early firearms, to freebond warehouses in Europe or leading international museums.

In recent years it has become an increasingly attractive option to become a private dealer: a business that is run on a by-appointment basis has far lower overheads than one centred on a retail outlet. The advent of the fax machine has contributed to this development, as has the ever-increasing ease of international air-travel. And while success as a private dealer doesn't come easy – it is dependent on expertise in the chosen subject, building a national or international reputation and good marketing skills – it can be highly lucrative.

For example, some top dealers (especially those who are trading in fine art) may only need to make a few sales a year to maintain a very high standard of living. The dealers that make up the sixth group in the network play a highly specialized role. Acting as consultants or agents they are employed by, for example, wealthy individuals or investment bodies (such as the trustees of pension funds), either to locate specific antiques or works of art, or to find buyers for them. They tend to be private collectors in their own right, have titled connections or have worked for one of the leading auction houses or museums. They make their money by charging a percentage of the sale price of the item(s) in question, but can do so only if the sale is successfully concluded. And while, unlike most other dealers, they do not have to invest their own money, or borrow it, to buy stock, they can run up quite substantial overheads – tsuch as ravel costs, accommodation, research, paperwork, etc. – in the course of tracking down particularly obscure or difficult-to-obtain pieces.

The seventh tier in the network is made up of a sizeable group consisting of 'trade only' dealers and warehouse exporters. Operating from unglamorous premises in the less well-heeled parts of town, they buy and sell antiques as if they were cans of beans or any other retail commodity. In that sense they fit perfectly Oscar Wilde's description of the 'man who knows the price of everything, but the value of nothing'.

Working very hard on tight cash-flows, and buying from auctions, street markets, antique fairs and house sales etc., they scrupulously assess each item when working out what to pay for it. Everything from condition, cost of restoration, transport, tax, ease of sale etc. is taken into account, and thus, in many respects, they can be considered the most professional dealers in the market place.

For example, you would never find one of them getting carried away during the bidding at an auction. Having worked out their price at the preview, they will stick to it rigidly, knowing that to do otherwise will reduce their profit when they come to sell. The more successful dealers in the group turn over millions of pounds worth of stock a year, most of their overseas clients (who are often dealers too) happily buying container loads of antiques without seeing them first.

The dealers who make up the eighth tier of the network own small shops selling both a wide range of antiques and collectables of variable quality. They also offer services such as picture framing or minor repairs and restorations as a side-line. A declining breed in major cities – the astronomical rise in leaseholds and rents over the past decade or two having forced them out of business – they are found mainly in the high streets of towns and villages on the tourist trail (overseas visitors providing them with their main source of income). Where they have survived in the cities is alongside the specialist dealers with stalls in antique markets, although they are few in number. Not always that knowledgeable about antiques, these small, general dealers are, however, invariably pleasant and helpful to potential customers, particularly those who know less about the subject than they do and are more interested in buying something that looks 'genuinely old', rather than whether it is authentically period.

The group below them are the regular open-market stallholders. In London, a typical example of this breed will have a stall in the Portobello Road or Bermondsey Market. Often specialising in a particular field, perhaps silver, prints or even something as obscure and specialised as kitchenware, he will scour the country during the week looking for items that he knows he will be able to sell, invariably for large wads of cash, to other dealers and collectors.

One of the key skills for this breed of dealer is to be able to keep their ears close to the ground and to know what is currently doing the rounds amongst the trade, which he would be interested in and where the best places are to snap up bargains. Stall holders may have to drive all round the country during the week (incurring enormous petrol bills en route) in search of interesting and attractive items for their stall, but, safe in the knowledge that it might well pay dividends. Furthermore, they will have many regular customers who will come and check out their stall every week and the dealer will want to give the impression he has a varied and fast-selling stock.

Below the stall-holders, at the bottom of the pile, are the 'runners'. With no premises to sell from, other than the boot and roof-rack of an old estate car, or the pavement, their overheads are mostly confined to petrol and other travel expenses. They buy from auctions, other dealers, in fact from anyone or anywhere that is selling something cheaper than it can be sold for somewhere else.

So, for example, if at one point in time pine chests are cheaper in the north of England than in the home counties, these dealers will 'run' them south to turn a profit. Their clients range from the top to the bottom of the dealer network, although they probably sell more pieces to the top West End dealers than anyone else in the trade. Selling strictly for cash, they tend to be far less burdened by taxation than most of their fellow professionals.

In addition to the main players described above, there are four other main sources and outlets for the buying and selling of antiques and collectables. How they work in practice is described in detail later in the book. However, it is important to note them briefly now, as they often play an important role in the sequence of transfers that can see an individual piece move from cheap, relative obscurity in the provinces to expensive prominence in a West End dealer's showroom.

First, there are the auction houses, which range in scale and status from the leading central London salerooms, such as Sotheby's, Christie's, Christie's South Kensington, Bonham's and Phillips, through the provincial auction rooms in other major cities and towns, to suburban and small-town auctions.

As a general rule, the bigger and more prestigious auction houses sell better-quality and more expensive antiques. They also regularly hold specialist sales, such as fine furniture, ceramics or pictures, in addition to general sales. Smaller auction houses hold many, more general, sales consisting of a wide range of antiques.

However, they do hold a few specialist sales throughout the year too, in which it is not unusual to find high-quality and commensurably expensive pieces. At the bottom of the pile, in terms of status, are the auction rooms that hold weekly or fortnightly general sales which, for the most part, consist of stock not dissimilar to that found in junk shops: in other words, you are just as likely to come across second-hand cookers and freezers as antiques.

Second, there are junk shops. Often owned by dealers who specialize in house clearances after there has been a death in the family, they generally have a range of goods on offer, mainly consisting of old (second-hand) furniture and all manner of bric-a-brac. Of course, hidden away in all of that there may well a valuable antique or two.

Third, there are charity shops and jumble sales which, again, have for sale a wide range of cheaply priced second-hand goods, some of which may be antiques and collectables. And fourth, there are the boot fairs, which have proliferated over the past decade and can be found virtually every weekend in farmers' fields or open public spaces all over the country. At these, members of the public sell their personal effects from the boots of their cars.

The considerable publicity given to them in the national newspapers, following the purchase of seemingly insignificant looking items for a few pence, which have turned out to be worth thousands of pounds at auction, has, naturally, fuelled their popularity. There are numerous stories in the antiques trade of items that have been bought initially for a few pounds and gradually worked their way from dealer to dealer until eventually being sold to a member of the public for tens or hundreds of thousands of pounds. However, I shall illustrate this phenomena with a personal anecdote that I am able to relate only because of a number of unlikely coincidences:

Many years ago I was looking for some reasonably priced furniture to go in a Georgian townhouse we had bought in Petworth, West Sussex. Having made a list of the pieces I needed, and the prices I was prepared to pay, I went along to a viewing at the local King & Chasemore auction salerooms in Pulborough. Walking in I noticed an interesting early Georgian bureau bookcase in need of some restoration. It was quite distinctive, being very narrow and displaying a particularly fine patina. Although it wasn't exactly what I was looking for, I marked it down as a possible buy if it went quite cheaply. On the day of the sale there was considerable interest in the bookcase, a number of people were bidding and it eventually went for £1,300 – far more than I could afford at the time.

Discussing the sale with a couple of local dealers later on, I was told they had found out the bookcase had originally been discovered during a house clearance on a farm in the north of England, and that the dealer had sold it to a runner who had brought it south and sold it on to another local dealer. As he was suffering from a severe cash-flow problem, he had put it into the auction at King & Chasemore, rather than restore it and await a buyer.

A few days later I was visiting the shop of a dealer friend in Tenterden, in Kent, when yet another dealer pulled up in his van and said he'd picked up an interesting piece at the auction the other day. Opening up the back of his van he revealed, surprise, surprise, the very same Georgian bookcase. After the usual negotiations my friend became its new owner, having paid £2,300 for the privilege. While we were admiring the piece, which was still standing in the driveway, another dealer arrived for a social chat. When he spotted the bookcase, he immediately offered £2,800 for it, which was quickly accepted.

Some weeks later I had to go to the workshops of the bookcase's new owner to pick up a chest he had restored for me. There in a corner was 'my' bookcase, having undergone a sensitive restoration and looking much smarter than when I last set eyes on it. I enquired the price, and he told me that he had already sold it for £3,600 to an Italian dealer who was known to be a runner for the London trade.

I then lost touch with my bookcase, although I did hear that instead of going directly to London it did have a short sojourn in Westerham, in Kent. However, some 18 months later I was hurrying along Bond Street to a Sotheby's sale when I spotted a wonderful bureau bookcase through the window of a shop. As with meeting a friend who has just had a very expensive face-lift, I did not immediately recognize the piece, which now had silk tassels hanging from the drawer keys. What else could I do, but go inside and have a closer look. After ringing the bell and being 'checked out' by the receptionist, I was ushered into the inner sanctum, and there, under the spotlights, was undoubtedly my friend from Pulborough.

The ticket hanging from one of the keys extolled the virtues of this early and rare piece, which seemed to have acquired a few secret compartments and a rather more intricate interior. There was, of course, no price displayed. So, having found a rather effete young male assistant, I asked how much it was. With a toss of his hair, and in the certain knowledge that I wouldn't be able to afford it, he replied: 'It is £35,000 actually, madam'.

There are a number of lessons to be learned from this tale. First and foremost, not only is it possible to make money out of antiques, but it is also possible, indeed quite common, for a number of people to make money on the same antique. Second, the price anyone can charge for an antique depends on who they know, who they are, where they are, and who their clients are. (In Chapter Six I will be discussing in detail the various options open to you if you wish to sell.) And third, if you want to make money - very good money - out of antiques you have to know your subject; more specifically, you have to know what you're looking at. In Chapter Two, I will show you the best ways of acquiring the necessary knowledge and expertise.

CHAPTER TWO

LEARNING ABOUT
ANTIQUES

——————— £ ———————

Unless you're extremely lucky you won't make money out of antiques without first becoming knowledgeable about the subject. Indeed most mistakes – often costly ones – are made as a result of ignorance. So, it is essential that you are able to recognize what something is, and develop an instinct or an 'eye' for whether it is 'right' – in other words, be able to spot whether it is genuine, reproduction or fake.

You must also be able to detect any repairs and restoration that may have been done, and know the effect these might have on the value of something. In addition, you have to know what is the right price to pay and the right price to sell for at any given time. And, finally, you should be able to sniff out a bargain and be able to avoid a rip-off.

Sadly, there are no short-cuts to becoming knowledgeable about antiques, particularly the process of educating your eye or building a feel for style. However, it is possible to set about it in a systematic, efficient and, perhaps most important of all, enjoyable way, so that you can begin buying and selling with a fair degree of confidence sooner rather than later.

As with many things in life, you should start with theory, rather than the practice. There are hundreds of books published on antiques, ranging from the general to the specialist, and a selection of suitable titles is listed under the heading 'Further Reading' at the back of this book. Most are available from book shops or public libraries. Titles that are no longer in print can often be found in good antiquarian booksellers too. I suggest you begin with a large encyclopedia, which will give you an overview of antiques as a whole, but bear in mind their limitations: they tend to illustrate and describe only the best, museum-quality pieces. Next, move on to some of the smaller-scale general titles, which provide more detailed information on the various subjects. There are three Miller's publications which you will find particularly instructive at this stage: *Understanding Antiques*, *Antiques and Collectables: The Facts At Your Fingertips* and *The Antiques Fact File*.

Once you have discovered some broad areas that you find especially interesting – such as furniture, porcelain, clocks, silverware, glass, jewelry, etc. – move on to the specialist books that cover these subjects in much greater detail. The *Miller's Antiques Checklist* series, for example, is specifically designed for this purpose, each title being dedicated to a particular subject, such as furniture, porcelain, Art Nouveau, Art Deco, dolls and teddy bears, silver and Sheffield Plate, etc. In addition to colour pictures, labelled diagrams and accompanying text, many of these titles also contain illustrated lists of the makers' marks and symbols that you find on many antiques, such as ceramics and silverware. These lists are an essential aid to identification when you actually come across the pieces out there in the real world.

Beyond the above are the numerous specialist titles, often written by academics, museum curators and leading collectors or dealers, that cover very specific subjects in minute and often in fascinating detail; typical and diverse examples include: Staffordshire portrait figures, English delftware, European treen, bamboo furniture, 18th-century English drinking glasses, etc. If you are to become really expert in a particular field, these are the sorts of titles that you will need to read. In addition to books, various magazines and periodicals often include useful articles on antiques and fine art. Suitable publications include: *The Antique Collector*, *The Antiques Trade Gazette*, *The Art Journal*, *Apollo*, *Country Life*, *The Magazine of Art* (1878-1904) and *The Studio* (1893-1960s). Issues of the last two, which have ceased publication, can be found in many of the larger public lending libraries, and museum archives. *The Antiques Trade Gazette*, which is available on subscription via your local newsagent, is also indispensable, because it lists all the forthcoming auction sales throughout the country.

Auction catalogues from the leading auction houses, such as Sotheby's and Christie's, are also useful, especially when they record sales of important collections. Often illustrated in colour, they allow you to study many examples of particular antiques and collectables at one time, and usually include estimated prices. However, they can be very expensive. Some of the larger catalogues can cost in the region of £25 each. Current issues are available from the auction houses themselves (names and addresses are listed at the back of the book). Back issues are in some cases held by the auction house. (At Christie's these can be viewed by appointment in their archives). In addition, the Victoria & Albert Museum and the National Art Library, in London, both hold major collections of old catalogues.

Keeping abreast of current prices in auctions and antique shops is obviously vital if you are going to buy or sell. *Miller's Antiques Price Guide*, *Miller's Collectables Price Guide* and *Miller's Picture Price Guide*, are published annually and designed for this purpose. However, factors such as the variation in prices from region to region, and price fluctuations from auction to auction (depending on who's bidding), mean that they must be used exactly as they are described: as guides to prices, not bibles. In addition to giving you useful ball park prices for a vast range of antiques, they are equally invaluable as visual references: the thousands of pictures of all manner of antiques are accompanied by useful captions with descriptions of each item – knowing what something is called, and learning the names of its various components is just as essential as knowing the right price if you want to trade in antiques.

While learning about antiques and collectables from the printed page is an essential step on the road to buying and selling, looking at them in the flesh and actually handling them is even more important if you are to develop a feel for style and an 'eye' for what is 'right'. Museums are a good place to start. Not only are many of them – local, national and international – treasure troves of antiques, they also employ knowledgeable and enthusiastic staff who are only too willing to provide expert information on the displays and collections. Many museums also give free opinions or attributions on objects taken in by members of the public. However, you must make an appointment and they are unlikely to offer valuations.

It is important to remember that the antiques you will find in museums (and stately homes open to members of the public, which are also worth visiting) are usually among the finest examples of their kind, and are usually in pristine condition. Consequently, it is best to view them as a benchmark against which you can judge more ordinary pieces you come across later on in private hands or in the trade.

Of course, one thing you can't do in museums and stately homes is actually handle the antiques. Touching them, picking them up, closely scrutinizing their various components is very important. There are a number of outlets that give you the opportunity to do this. Sale previews at auction houses are ideal; usually held the day or the morning before the sale itself, they are attended by both members of the trade and public, who are able to inspect the lots at their leisure. Entry is free, although you may have to buy a catalogue, which you should do in any case as they contain pictures and descriptions of the lots together with estimated price guides.

Chapter Three (see pages 34-87) covers what you should be looking for with particular antiques, but for now, the best advice I can give is: having inspected an item at close quarters, stand back and look at it as a whole. Assessing factors such as colour, shape and proportion from a distance is the best way of telling if something is 'right' or authentic, as opposed to fake or improperly restored. Developing an 'eye' for this takes time. However, the more you do it, and the more knowledgeable you become, the easier it becomes. Also, remember that there are usually staff on hand to answer any questions you might have.

Estimated prices in auction catalogues have to be treated with care. They relate only to the object itself and don't (can't) take into account who will be bidding for it. You only need two people in the saleroom to be really keen on a lot for it to fetch a sum well above its estimated price. Similarly, lack of interest can result in something going for much less than the estimate or, having failed to reach its reserve, being 'bought in' by the auction house. (A description of how lots are bought and sold at auction can be found in Chapters Four and Six.)

So, to get a feel for the prices that pieces are actually bought and sold for, you should attend the auction itself – in fact, go to as many as possible. Don't buy anything at this stage. Instead, mark down in your catalogue the price each lot fetches as it goes under the hammer. Price depends in part on condition, so it's important to have also noted this in your catalogue during the preview.

As well as attending auctions and auction previews, you can learn a tremendous amount about antiques and collectables by looking at them on market stalls, at antique fairs, and in antique shops. Again, you should be able to touch or pick up pieces for closer inspection. However, don't take this for granted and always ask the owner of the stall or shop first. You'll find that most dealers are only too happy to answer questions if you sound interested. And, it is also worth remembering, from their viewpoint you might be an important collector in-the-making, with whom they could build up a long-term and profitable relationship

Over the years I have found that cultivating a good relationship with a dealer, or better still a number of dealers, is one of the best ways of learning about antiques. Specialist dealers in particular are incredibly knowledgeable about their subject and, out of necessity, are very *au fait* with current prices. However, unlike museums they don't provide a public service. So, if you want to talk to them purely for the purposes of acquiring information, either try to make an appointment or pick a moment when they aren't busy with a potential customer. There is nothing more annoying and off-putting for a dealer than to be plagued with a stream of endless questions while he or she is trying to earn a living.

Treating antique dealers insensitively, taking them for granted, or just appearing plain stupid may well result in an unhelpful response. For example, I remember an art dealer from Durban, South Africa, bending my ear about how some members of the general public tended to ask the imossible. Telephone enquiries along the lines of : 'How much is my painting with three cows, two people and some hills in the distance worth?', were, believe it or not, surprisingly common. After hours of patiently responding in a helpful and professional manner: 'Is it oil or watercolour?', he decided enough was enough, and changed tack. Conversations now went along the lines of: 'Are they steep hills?...good. Now, are the two people sitting or standing?...great. But which way are the cows facing?...Oh, to the left (right). What a shame, there's not much call for left- (right-) facing cows these days.' The dealer said it might have cost him a few masterpieces, but it was definitely worth it in the long run.

The best type of dealers to cultivate (tactfully) in your search for knowledge are the ones who have been established for quite some time, and have an academic and not just a commercial enthusiasm for the subjects in which they specialise. One way of getting in touch with them is via B.A.D.A. (The British Antique Dealers' Association), or L.A.P.A.D.A. (The Association of Art and Antique Dealers). Their addresses are listed at the back of the book, and both organisations publish a list of members which indexes dealers by his or her name and speciality and where he or she is based.

However good the advice you receive, you should always remember that identifying antiques can sometimes be a rather imprecise science. There are some pieces that even the leading experts can't agree on. I remember working a few years ago with a leading furniture specialist from one of the top London auction houses. I told him that I still found furniture the most difficult area in which I could be absolutely sure that what I was looking at was what it was supposed to be. I'd just spent two weeks in Williamsburg in the United States and had watched expert local craftsmen use seasoned wood, old tools and pattern books by Chippendale and Sheraton to 'recreate' period chairs. They were so well done I was sure that, once they had naturally aged a bit, I would have had considerable difficulty in telling them apart from originals made c.1770.

The specialist admitted that this was a real problem, and that some months before he had received a phone call from the owners of a large country house who wanted discretely to sell some antiques, including a pair of early chairs that were mentioned in an inventory of the house compiled in 1760. He went down to see them and immediately thought they were exceptional, but also felt something was wrong. He couldn't say what it was, it was just a gut feeling. Despite this, he took them back to the auction house in London and let other members of his department have a look. They all thought, however, that the chairs were absolutely right. Only one dealer, who had dropped in on another matter, queried their authenticity, but he could only back this up by saying they just felt wrong.

At the next important furniture auction the chairs had been catalogued as a fine and rare pair of George I chairs, and duly sold for well over £10,000. Who was right? The only definitive answer you can give is that the chairs were probably authentic – well at least two people bidding in the room thought so. In Chapter Three I've described what to look out for with particular types of antiques, so that you can at least maximize your chances of being right.

WHAT TO LOOK FOR

———————— £ ————————

Not long after I first started buying antiques a dealer pointed out to me there are more English oak refectory tables in antique shops, auctions and homes around the world than there were houses in 16th-century England of a sufficient size to even get them through the front door. In other words, fakes and forgeries abound in the world of antiques. As Herbert Cescinsky wrote in the 1920s in *The Gentle Art of Faking Furniture*: 'There is more English antique furniture exported to America and Europe in one year than could have been made in the whole of the 18th century' – a trade (now two-way) that continues to this day and is by no means limited to furniture. There's an old joke in the world of fine art about the fact that there are one thousand genuine Rembrandts in the world, and two thousand of those are in America. (Of course, this is not particularly funny, and rather costly, if you're on the receiving end of the con.)

Using traditional tools and techniques, together with various tricks of the trade, craftsmen and artists around the world reproduce 'original antiques' or doctor or repair existing pieces often to such a high standard that it can be extremely difficult for even an expert with years of experience to distinguish between them and genuine originals. However, with most fakes and forgeries there are usually one or two tell-tale signs that can reveal when a particular piece is not all its cracked up to be, and you will need to be able to recognise them if you want to make money out of antiques – authentic and original pieces invariably command higher sums than both forgeries (provided that the latter are detected) and poorly repaired or altered ones. (However, given the everyday wear and tear most antiques are subjected to, some of the repairs are inevitable and unavoidable, and, if well-executed, need not dramatically affect the value of a piece.)

The signs of forgery, alteration, repair and restoration can vary from incorrect maker's marks (as with ceramics and metal wares) to wrong proportions and method of construction and uneven patination (as with furniture).

There is a number of specialist titles on the market, notably Miller's *Understanding Antiques*, which cover this subject in greater detail than space here allows (they are listed under 'Further Reading' at the back of the book). However, in this chapter I have outlined some of the most important things that, in my experience, you should know about and be looking out for all the time.

FURNITURE

Repairs

Given that furniture is subject to everyday wear and tear and can be quite easily damaged, it is not surprising that many antiques have had to be repaired at one time or another. Provided such repairs have been carried out sympathetically they need not detract in any significant way from the value of a piece; however, crude and unskilled ones will.

In addition to the replacement of worn or damaged parts, acceptable repairs include, for example, the stripping of coats of paint applied at a later date, together with the removal of French polish applied by the Victorians in the 19th century over the original finish.

Alterations and Restoration

Many alterations were made simply to conform a piece to changing fashions, personal taste or individual domestic requirements (such as to fit into a specific space). For example, tallboys were often split to make two chests, with a top added to the base piece and feet to the top.

Early 18th-century walnut pieces altered in this manner can be very valuable in their own right. Such alterations can often be detected by the presence of saw marks on rails, stretchers or backs. Other, so-called, improvements, particularly those which were made during the 19th century by the Victorians, include embellishing existing legs and feet, carving the original plain wood, replacing tops and doors, re-veneering and adding inlaid or carved panels.

The Victorians also cut down large Tudor or Elizabethan pieces to fit into their dining rooms and parlours – the presence of new frame members and saw marks on the panelling are an indication of such alterations.

While most of these improved pieces are now judged to be antiques in their own right, they are less valuable than the unmodified originals. The general rule with all antiques is that they will hold their value better if in good condition and with all their original components.

Marriages

Unions, or marriages, of two pieces (such as a writing bureau and a bookcase) are quite common and were (and are) done to produce a more saleable (and valuable) two-part piece. If the two original pieces are of the same period, the result, provided it is well done and openly sold as a marriage, is perfectly acceptable, although this should be reflected in a lower price.

You should always look very carefully at two-part pieces for signs of a marriage. Check that the carcass wood, veneer, colour, proportions and general 'feel' match top and bottom. Different styles of construction for the base and top indicate a marriage, as do old screw holes in the base which do not match up with the top. Original tops were made smaller so that they could fit within a moulding on the top of the base. Also, the base top, being hidden, would not have been veneered. If a top sits flush on the base, or the base top is veneered, you are invariably looking at a marriage. The best place to assess whether a piece is a marriage is from the back: if the back-boards top and bottom don't match, check all the above.

Copies

Numerous copies of 18th-century pieces were produced during the 19th century. Many of these were skilfully made with high-quality materials. Given that they have also aged naturally by now it can be quite difficult to distinguish them from original examples. However, many examples are noticeably heavier in terms of construction and execution. Also, while old wood was frequently used for these copies, Victorian saw marks on panels often give the game away. The presence of French polish, which didn't come into general use until the 19th century, is also a good indicator of its age.

It is important to remember that many reproductions or copies of earlier pieces made during the 19th century were never intended to deceive. Indeed, copies of Georgian and Regency furniture made in the second quarter of the century are sought after in their own right nowadays. Moreover, many late 19th-century and modern copies were made and sold 'in the style of', rather than as exact replicas. Consequently, they are not difficult to distinguish from the original.

Fakes

Unlike copies or reproductions, fakes were, and are, made to be (fraudulently) passed off as originals. While you should check the specific things to watch out for different types of furniture listed later in the chapter, the following general flaws and discrepancies often reveal that a particular piece is not quite what it seems at first glance:

• Is the wood used correct for the piece and the period?
• Do any pieces of wood look too new? The edges of period timber at the back of a piece will often be blackened.
• Is the veneer hand- rather than machine-cut? (see below).
• If there is herringbone inlay, does it lie flat with the surrounding surface? The effects of humidity over time on an original piece cause the inlay to lift slightly proud of the surrounding area – a characteristic that is extremely difficult to simulate.
• Are the handles, escutcheons (plates around the handles), locks, screws and castors right for the piece and the period.
• Do the fittings look as if they have been attached since teh piece of furniture was originally made.
• Are any brass fittings original? Because of its higher copper

content, 18th-century brass has a softer feel and a more subtle colour than harder, brighter and more shiny modern brass – an effect that can not be duplicated.

•Do the patches of discoloration around the heads of screws and nails look authentic – this naturally occurring effect is difficult to simulate accurately.

•Does the grain on any beading on an 18th-century piece run true? Unlike Victorian and later beading it was produced from one piece of wood, rather than being glued on.

•Is the evidence of wear on stretchers, rails, doors convincing? Artificial distressing/ageing of areas subject to wear and tear is quite common, but difficult to reproduce authentically. If you don't think it looks right, it probably isn't.

•Are the proportions of the piece right? Step back and take a look. You have to develop an eye or feel for this and, again, if it doesn't look right, it probably isn't.

•Is the piece a pastiche? Many items of furniture have been substantially rebuilt, using some of the original parts, such as most of the carcass, in order to make them into another, more desirable (and valuable) piece. Better-known examples include dressing tables, kneehole desks, writing tables and commodes. It is also quite common to come across sets of eight chairs made, with some new parts, from five originals. Similarly, large pieces are often cut down to make smaller, more saleable, items such as tallboys, secretaires, chests-of-drawers and breakfront bookcases.

•Pastiches can look authentic at first glance. However, closer inspection of decoration, veneer, feet, drawers and fittings may reveal otherwise.

•Is any carving original? Original carving always stands proud of the surrounding area. Flat or incised carving has almost certainly been added later, as has shallow carving, and detracts from the value of the piece.

Patination

The layers of polish, dirt and grime that build up over time on the surface of wooden furniture combine to produce the lustrous patination that confers considerable value to a piece. While the colour of the patination will always vary depending on the underlying wood, it should be fairly uniform over the surface of the piece of furniture, except in the following areas:

• Those exposed to sunlight, where it will be lighter
• Those subject to constant handling, such as under drawer handles or the arms of chairs, or in the recesses of mouldings and carvings and other crevices, where it will be darker.

Authentic-looking patination is quite difficult to fake, even for an experienced craftsman, and therefore reasonably easy to spot. However, watch out for areas of heavily applied wax polish designed to conceal conversions or replacement parts.

Drawers

These are an important means of dating and authenticating antique furniture; their construction and furnishings (handles, escutcheons, etc.), and the type of wood used all provide important clues. However, it is important to remember that, as with most things, there are exceptions to the rule. For example, local craftsmen often amended basic designs, and what appeared in London in, say, 1810, might not have reached the provinces until three or four years later, while the other side of the Atlantic might be anything between 10 to 30 years behind.

17th Century

• Early 17th-century drawers were nailed together, the side runners fitting into deep side grooves.
• Runners were sometimes nailed to the side of the carcass on the inside.
• Original runners should show signs of wear, and many will have been replaced over the years.

•If the drawer handles are original the surrounding wood will be darker and possibly show slight indentations.

•From the mid-17th century, dovetails were often concealed by intricate mouldings (such as beading and reeding).

18th Century (Georgian)

•Drawer linings were made of oak until the mid-18th century.

•Good quality drawers had oak sides, with rounded top edges.

•Bottom boards were made from two or three pieces of the same wood, and grooved to form bottom runners.

•Up to 1770 the grain in bottom boards ran from front to back; after 1770 from side to side, often with a central bearer for extra support.

•No 18th-century drawers exactly fit the space between front and back – a space was always left for ventilation at the back.

19th Century

•Corner mouldings on drawers were introduced after 1790.

•The Victorians made bottom boards from one piece of wood, which was usually screwed to the sides.

•Machine-made dovetails show it is post-1880 (see below).

Hand-made   Machine-made

Checking Drawers

•Make sure the dovetailing in all drawers in a piece match.

•Check if the dovetails at the back of the drawer show signs of alteration – if so, the drawer has almost certainly been reduced in depth.

•Check the wood of the carcass is the same age as the base and back of the drawers. If it isn't, look at the rest of the piece.

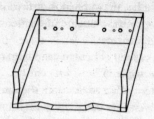

•Check if handles have been moved or changed; this may indicate a drawer has been reduced in width to fit a new piece. Look at the reverse of the front for filled holes (see above). If there are no corresponding holes on the front the veneer is almost certainly later than the drawer.

•If you ever find one example of a replacement, an alteration or a restoration on a piece, look elsewhere for others.

Veneers

Introduced in the early 18th century, veneers consist of a thin sheet of finely figured and grained, high-quality wood applied to the visible (or show) surfaces of furniture, the carcass of which was made of a coarser, cheaper wood. Veneers helped to mask the construction of the piece, and were cut to display the grain in a highly decorative manner that was impossible with solid wood.

•Early veneers were always hand-cut, with a minimum thickness of approximately 1.5mm (¹⁄₁₆th in) and more commonly around 3mm (¹⁄₈th in). Consequently, any veneer uniformly thinner has been machine-cut in the early 19th century.

•If a carcass is genuine 18th-century, then any veneer thinner than 1.5mm (¹⁄₁₆th in) was either added considerably later, or the piece has been re-veneered.

•Early 18th-century oak furniture was often embellished with a later, walnut veneer.

•If a veneered piece has drawers, look at the inside front of the drawer. Part of this should be made of the coarser carcass softwood if the veneer is original.

•If the inside front is solid oak, then any veneer was almost certainly added late, possible in the 19th century..

•Cross-cut veneers set at an angle of 45 degrees indicate a date of late 17th century or very early 18th century. This is also true of cross-grain combined with herringbone configurations. Cross-grain banding alone usually indicates a date after 1710.

•Feather-banding on drawers should be continuous.

•Watch out for plain veneers on an otherwise decorated piece. These could indicate replacement of the original veneer.

•Inspect hinges on doors. If the areas around them are unusually free of dirt and grime the veneer has probably been steamed off to repair the carcass wood below, and replaced.

•Hand-cut veneers show saw marks when viewed from above, machine-cut veneers look much smoother.

•19th-century machine-cut veneers are wafer thin and exhibit very little figuring.

•If a bubble in a veneer can be easily pressed in with a finger it is either machine-cut, or the surface has been sanded down, probably to obliterate signs of damage.

•A great number of pieces have, at one time or another, been re-veneered. This reduces their value significantly.

Marquetry

An extension of veneering, marquetry is the art of inlaying elaborate designs in different coloured woods or graining, or other materials such as ivory or various metals. Originating in Europe, it was particularly popular in the Netherlands from the end of the 17th century.

•Watch out for pieces where a marquetry panel was applied later - originals have raised edges of glue or grain.

Beds

Few original four poster beds have survived. Most were rebuilt from the middle of the 19th century to fit smaller rooms and taller people.

•Skilfully lengthened or widened examples can be more valuable than shorter narrower originals, provided they retain their original components and have compatible additions.

•Additional decorations can detract from the value.

•Beds which retain their original drapes are both rare and valuable. Replacement is a costly business.

•Because so many original cradles have survived intact, repaired examples fetch much lower prices.

Bookcases

The glazing bars in glass-fronted bookcases should match the rest of the piece in terms of quality, timber used and age.

•A bureau-bookcase should have three separate components: bureau base, bookcase and pediment. The veneers on all three should match.

•The bookcase component of a bureau-bookcase should be slightly smaller than the base, with a moulding fitted to the base, not the top. The top of the base should not be veneered. The sides of the base and bookcase should not be flush or joined. If they are this could indicate a 'cut-down' from a larger library bookcase. The backs of the base and bookcase should match for wood, patination and colour. If the handles and escutcheons are out of proportion, the piece could have been made up from a larger piece.

•Many breakfront bookcases were originally 19th-century breakfront wardrobes. Watch out for signs of anything up to 20cm (8ins) having been cut off the depth, and check the glazing in the frames are of the correct period.

•Some bookcases have been reduced in height and have had

pediments added at a later date, often in the mid-19th century.

•Pairs of dwarf bookcases (which are supposedly late 18th-century, Regency and Federal) were sometimes constructed from one large, original bookcase.

Bureaux

Size is critical to value: bureaux fetch considerably more if under 96.5cm (38in) in width; 91.5cm (36in) is considered to be the ideal width.

•Bureaux cabinets are prone to marriage or separation. A bureau intended to bear a cabinet will normally have a steeper fall than one intended to stand alone. The retaining moulding should be on the top of the bureau, not on the foot of the cabinet – the latter suggests a possible marriage.

•Many bureaux were reduced in width to increase their value. Look for multiple sets of screw holes on the inside of the drawer fronts where handles have been realigned.

•Many Victorian oak bureaux were veneered to be passed off as Regency ones. Look for back panels of unveneered oak, mahogany or pine planking. Also look at the inside of drawers: original pieces should have a top lip of oak with pine below – solid oak usually indicated later veneering.

•Avoid any bureaux with cracks and splits, particularly to the flap and sides, and any with replaced flaps.

Cabinets and Sideboards

Early examples are more elegant and harmonious in terms of proportion and decoration than many of the over-richly decorated examples produced from the mid 19th century onwards.

•Size affects value: many early examples were quite deep, but narrower examples under 122cm (4ft) are better suited to modern rooms and therefore are more in demand. Consequently, watch out for cut-down originals (often revealed by a join on the top undersurface of the cabinet or sideboard).

•The central drawer of sideboards should be baize-lined with compartments, and side drawers or cupboards should have containers – their removal reduces value.

•The tops of early sideboards should be made of one timber; sideboards with two- or three-piece tops are often Victorian.

•In the early 20th century, cabinets were commonly made from wardrobes. Watch out for the presence of drawers instead of cupboards, a low base in proportion to the top, modern glass and adjustable shelving on ladders.

•Many Victorian chiffoniers were mass-produced and made to look like earlier pieces (notably Regency) by the addition of gilt mounts, brass grilles and pleated silk fronts.

•When damaged, the wooden tops of chiffoniers were often replaced with marble. Their subsequent value depends on the quality and general attractiveness of the marble.

•Many cabinets were converted from chests, bookcases and wardrobes. One tell-tale sign is incorrect proportions when the piece is viewed as a whole.

Canterburies

Square legs are an indication of an early example; round, tapered and turned legs did not appear until c.1810.

•The first Canterburies were made as plate holders to stand by the table. They were later used to hold sheet music.

•The highest prices are paid for rare shapes, crisp deep carving and decorations which feature attractive musical motifs (such as lyre sides).

•Watch out for examples made from cut-down whatnots or étagères. These will show signs of new parts and re-finishing.

•Many modern reproductions abound. However, they will always lack patination and their turned parts are too regular to be genuine pieces.

Commodes

Highly decorative examples fetch the highest prices, particularly if features such as finely figured veneers and marquetry and escutcheons look integral to the piece and help to articulate its shape and outline.

•Later copies tend to be more elaborately decorated and scaled down to suit smaller rooms.

•Signs of 19th- and 20th-century reproductions include regular machine-cut dovetailing on the drawers and steam-shaped softwood carcasses with very thin veneers.

Chairs

Numerous different chair designs have been produced over the centuries. However, so many copies of earlier chairs were made during the 19th century you have to be very careful to ensure earlier chairs are genuine.

•Watch out for signs of natural wear and tear on the chair's feet, back and seat.

•If the stretcher rails seem too close to the ground, the legs may have been shortened because the feet have worn. So long as the seat is at least 46cm (18ins) from the ground this need not affect the value.

•Repairs can reduce value, so watch out for new parts – their patination may be different from the rest of the chair.

•Solid corner blocks in seat frames, if fixed with screws, are either replacements for originals or indicate the chair is a copy.

•Copies of armchairs made in the 19th century usually have back panels of an even thickness, a uniform dark varnish, carved arms, and stretchers which are exactly the same distance from the ground.

•19th-century copies of 17th- or 18th-century armchairs which had carved backs and seats often have upholstery instead.

•Many armchairs made after 1730 have a back splat which fits into a shoe which is separate from the back seat rail. If the shoe and the rail are made from one piece of timber, then the chair is a 19th-century copy. The same applied to dining chairs.

•The legs and arms of armchairs are the most frequently replaced pieces. Check them carefully for different patination.

•Original upholstery is rare, and if in good condition increases the value of a piece substantially. Be careful of deep buttoning: it should be to the back of the armchair only, and stop at the 'waist-line', where the arms join the back.

•Early mahogany dining chairs have a silky feel. This is because the mahogany was oiled smooth, not varnished.

•Many 19th-century copies can be quite valuable, but avoid those with skimpy legs.

•Watch out for scrambled sets. This is where one or more members are replaced in each chair to make up new ones to increase the number in a set. This practise is widespread.

•Watch out that re-upholstered drop-in seats have not forced the frame apart and damaged the leg/seat rail junctions.

Chests

Genuine pre-Jacobean and 17th-century coffers are made from split or quarter-sawn timbers with rounded edges. They never show saw marks and any splintering along the grain will have worn smooth with age.

•The lids of genuine early coffers should be bowed or curved with shrinkage between the planks. They will also usually have worn feet, panels loose from shrinkage and good patination inside the lid from handling.

•Watch out for early unadorned coffers that were carved in the 19th century. The carving will have relatively sharp edges.

•To identify repairs to and copies of chests of drawers, refer to the section on drawers on page 00. But also note that: drawers without locks will be 19th century or later; a top flight of three drawers means the chest was once the top half of a tallboy; late 17th-century and 18th-century chests of drawers tend to be lighter than 19th-century ones and they also tend to be smaller.

•Watch out for Georgian chests that were re-veneered and inlaid in the 19th century with thin lifeless veneer.

•Watch out for marriages of unrelated pieces to create chests-on-stands. Check the dovetailing of the drawers, the back panels, veneers and any decoration match on both pieces.

•Original feet and handles add to the value of a piece, and also help with dating it.

Cupboards

Two-tier court cupboards may have been cut down from three-tier ones. Check the top timber is the same age as the rest and shows no sign of dowel holes. Also, the reverse may have happened: i.e. a three-tier from a two-tier. Look for differences in colour and hardness of timber, plus decorative inconsistencies. Victorian copies lack the patination, hardness and wear of earlier examples.

•All pre-Victorian corner cupboards were backed in unfinished wood and painted. Look for signs of the original paint.

•Avoid Regency clothes presses that have been gutted inside to make wardrobes.

•Most dressers on the market today have been repaired, then wire-brushed and polished to look original. So, check all the timbers have consistent colour, patination and hardness.

Desks

All good desks are rock solid. Any piece that isn't is either second-rate or a marriage.

•The best are made of close-grained hardwoods. Veneered softwood desks deteriorate quickly – the veneer usually lifts.

•Because kneehole desks are in great demand there are numerous fakes and conversions around. The versions with four, as opposed to six, bracket feet are easiest to fake by converting a chest of drawers.

•Check the inner sides of the pedestals for veneers that do not match the rest of the piece. Also check inside the carcass around the drawer opening for lack of wear to the kneehole side. And check the frieze between the pedestals for saw marks which might indicate recent manufacture.

•A brushing slide (a pull-out pull-in piece) in a kneehole desk might also indicate a conversion; they are more commonly found on a flat writing surface. Finally, a kneehole desk which has drawers to one side is almost certainly a converted Victorian washstand.

•Also look for evidence of replaced desk supports, rising top and drawers knobs. In particular, a plain writing top may have been replaced with a piano top in order to increase the value of the piece.

•Pedestal desks are built in three sections, and are therefore susceptible to marriages of unrelated parts. Check veneer and colour consistency, plus solidity of the piece as a whole.

•The tops were often replaced with solid wood. Original examples should always have stud-fixed leather panels (three on a large desk) in a frame of cross-cut veneer with an overhanging lip moulding.

•Any tooled leather panels are late 19th or 20th century.

•Original tops are ideal, but a good replacement is better than a bad old one. Some early pedestal desks were cut down to suit changing fashions – you can detect a reduction in length by the handle repositioning on the central drawer; reduction in depth can be ascertained by feeling for a cut in the desk top.

•Some damaged kneehole desks were adapted to pedestals. These can be detected by looking for new timber and veneer on the inner face of the pedestal.

•Mass-produced, fake Regency pedestals are revealed by thin, cheap veneers applied to the wrong carcass wood – i.e. something other than mahogany or baywood (and sometimes oak).

•As desks have always been sought after, you will find there are far more reproductions, improved, married and faked desks than genuine period pieces on the market.

Dumb Waiters

Dumb waiters are easy to adapt to a more desirable piece. Marriages are common, so check for differences in turning between the different column sections. Two-tier pieces may have been cut down from a three-tier example, or made from unrelated parts. Check for inconsistent turning, and step back and see if the proportions look right. Examples that feel light, lack patina and have shallow carving are probably 19th-century or later copies.

Early Oak Furniture

Oak was the principal material for all furniture up to c.1670, and well into the 19th century for country furniture. When assessing if an early piece is genuine, look for the following:

•Originally a golden honey colour, early oak will have aged to a warm chestnut to black colour, with a rich patination from centuries of polish and handling.

•Wear and tear is inevitable, but avoid very badly damaged pieces as repair is expensive.

•Avoid pieces which have been embellished at a later date. Any Victorian carving will be in relief with sharp edges. Original carving stands proud and will be smooth, any late veneering and inlay will be thin machine-cut, and often displays inappropriate patterns.

•Mass-produced 19th-century oak pieces were often made of poorly seasoned timber, which usually splits and only looks old to an inexperienced eye. So, check carefully for black lines in the grain, saw marks on hidden edges, thin timbers and machine carving. However, well-made 19th-century oak pieces can fetch good prices and are often just as appealing.

•Oak tables can be dated fairly accurately by their legs and stretchers. Late examples are often revealed by heavy bulbous mouldings or over elaborate imitations of earlier styles, such as barley-sugar twist.

•Always avoid tables that have been cut down, which lack patination to the cut edges.

•Oak chests should be checked carefully for brass pins. This is usually a sign that the piece is 19th century, or that the mouldings have been added at a later date.

Mirrors

Pre-1773 looking glass was blown from a cylinder of glass, which thus limited its size. Thus early mirrors are either small, or made of two or three pieces covered by astragal bars at the joins. After 1773, it was possible to make large single mirrors.

•Old glass has a different reflective quality to modern glass: the image is dark rather than luminous, and when viewed at an angle has a grey rather than a green tone. Early glass is also thinner at the top of the frame than the bottom, and thinner overall than modern glass.

•You can check the thickness by placing the point of a pencil on the glass and looking at the distance between the point and its image. A short distance indicates old glass, and vice-versa.

•Be suspicious of any mirror which is still in perfect condition. All old mirrors will have deteriorated over the years and have non-reflective spots.

•19th century frames tended to be of stucco built up on a wire frame. Some are excellent, but worth considerably less if the stucco is cracked with age.

Stools

Make sure that the legs have not been replaced with staircase balusters in an attempt to enhance the value.

• Tops are often replaced. Be suspicious of an absence of shine due to wear, or if there is no sign of damage or shrinkage.

• Hessian under an upholstered seat indicates a post-1840 date, or might conceal alterations on an earlier piece.

Tables

Genuine oak refectory tables are one or two planks wide, never three. None have survived without repair. In terms of value, replacement of stretchers or feet are less important than loss of the original legs, bearers or top. Reproductions all have sawn tops, not split, and regular machine-made dowels. Their legs have exaggerated mouldings and large melon-shaped bulbs. Watch out for tops made from old floorboards. These will have holes (possibly filled) where they were nailed to joists.

• Early side tables should be well patinated on the underside of the top. Lack of patination indicates a Victorian copy.

• The flaps of gate-leg tables should be at least 2.5cm (1in) thick, made from a single piece of timber and be uneven in thickness due to hand-cutting. Copies are made of thinner timber with uniformly regular turning.

• A period lowboy with only one drawer, instead of three, may be a side table with an added frieze.

• The underframe of early drop-leaf tables should be made of oak or red pine, and the top of heavy mahogany at least 2.5cm (1in) thick. Lighter mahogany may indicate a Victorian copy.

• Any original carving on an early card table should stand proud of the curve of the cabriole legs, not within the outline.

• Occasional tables are often faked, restored and reproduced. Many period drinks trays were married to a base from a firescreen. So, check the underside of the tray for inappropriate distressing and breaks in the column grain. If present, these indicate the shaft is from another piece and has been given a collar for extra height.

•Some sofa tables are in fact marriages of a period top to a cheval mirror stand. Look for supports set too close, a turned stretcher with a square block and disguised screw holes.

•The commonest type of 'improvement' to a table is the cutting of a round or oval top from a square one. So, always check the underside patination is continuous. There should also be a minimum overhang of 5cm (2in) between the legs and the outer edge.

•Filled holes, signs of previous fixings and un-oxidised areas where timbers have been removed all indicate repair or modification to a table, and should be treated with caution.

Walnut Furniture

Walnut is especially prone to woodworm and, being relatively soft, easily splits. Avoid damaged pieces.

•Early walnut is not the same as 'black' or Virginia walnut. Some later 17th-century/early 18th-century pieces were made in the latter, but it was mostly used after 1830.

•Walnut is easily carved. Characteristically, early walnut furniture has twist-turned legs and detailed mouldings.

Wine Coolers

Avoid coolers in poor condition or with replaced mounts. (The absence of the old lead lining is less serious.)

•Coolers of coopered construction are more common than jointed forms. Round, oval, hexagonal and octagonal shapes are all found in coopered form.

•The earliest coolers have plain square or turned, tapering legs. After 1800, large carved paw feet are more common, and the sarcophagus shape became popular.

PORCELAIN AND POTTERY

The three most important things to learn in this field are:
• The distinction between pottery and porcelain.
• The distinction between hard and soft paste porcelain.
• The distinction between hand-painted and printed wares.
There are numerous very useful specialist books on this subject, and I have listed some at the back of the back. However, the following should be of help:
• Pottery is not translucent, while porcelain is. You must bear in mind that some porcelains do have very little translucency.
• Hard paste porcelain feels cold to the touch and broken chips of it feel like flint or glass. It also has a hard, glittery glaze which is fused to the paste.
Soft paste porcelain has a warmer feel, and broken chips feel more granular. The glaze also tended not to fuse into the body as much as on hard porcelain, and therefore was liable to pooling and crazing; the earlier examples were also prone to occasional discoloration.
• The brush strokes of hand-painted porcelain are much more fluid than printed examples, especially in areas of shading. The brushwork is also less precise than an engraving.

Marks

All marks on pottery and porcelain should be viewed with suspicion. There are many good specialist books on the subject, which are well-worth investing in as they provide a comprehensive list. However, the following are useful tips on dating:
• Pattern numbers don't denote a specific factory, but tend to date from after 1815 and are usually much later.
• The marks, 'Limited' or 'Ltd', tends to denote a date after 1861, but became much more common after 1885.
• An impressed 'Trade Mark' can be assumed to be after 1862.

•The word 'Royal' in a firm's name implies late 19th century.

•From 1891 wares started to state the country of origin:

•'Bone China' and 'English bone China' are 20th-century pottery and porcelain marks.

•'Made in England', 'France', etc. implies it was made in the 20th century.

THE MAJOR FACTORIES

Bow (1744-75)
Blue and White
Early period 1749-54

•Often thickly potted. Glaze can be blue/green in pools. Many wares painted in pale clear royal blue, which sometimes blurs. Some well potted wares marked with an incised 'R'.

Middle period 1755-6

•Darker underglaze blue. More thinly potted but relatively heavy. Body more porous and prone to staining. Painter's numerals used on the base of the piece and sometimes inside footrings, as with Lowestoft.

Late period 1765-75

•Poor translucency and quality. Can resemble earthenware.

Bow Polychrome

•Early wares decorated in vivid famille rose colours.

•Patterns usually included chrysanthemum and peony.

•Earliest wares have greyish body. By 1754, a good ivory tone had been achieved.

•After 1760 colours can appear dull and dirty.

•In late 1750s some attractive botanical plates were produced, which are now highly sought after.

•After 1760 Meissen-influenced floral decoration is commonly found on Bow polychrome porcelain wares.

Bristol (c.1749-81)
Early Period c.1749-52
• Very rare porcelains, but sometimes show relief moulded marks 'Bristol' or 'Bristoll'.
• Mostly underglaze blue ware with chinoiserie decoration.
• Tight fitting glaze but a tendency to pool and bubble.
• The blue often looks watery where it has run in the firing.
• In 1752 Bristol moulds sold to Worcester.
• Very difficult to differentiate late Lund's Bristol from early Worcester porcelain wares.

Late Period c.1770-81
• Body has tendency to slight tears and firing cracks.
• Early wares very difficult to differentiate from Plymouth – both show smoky ivory glaze and wreathing in the body.
• Champion took over in 1773.
• Mid and late 1770s, the dominant decorative style was neo-classical – especially delicate swags and scattered flowers.
• Later pieces show imperfections in the enamel and potting.
• Later colours are sharp and gilding is of good quality.

Caughley (1772-1799)
• Painted wares tend to be earlier than printed ones.
• Bodies of the soapstone type shows orange to transmitted light, but can show greenish, which adds to the confusion with Worcester porcelain wares.
• Good, close fitting glaze, but when gathered in pools can have greeny-blue tint.
• From 1780s many pieces heightened in gilding.
• Often confused with Worcester. They have many patterns in common, such as 'The Cormorant and Fisherman' and 'Fence' patterns.
• However, hatched crescents never appeared on Caughley; they were purely a Worcester mark.

Chantilly (1725-1800)

•Up to 1750s had milk-white opaque tin-glaze.

•Beautiful white finish inspired by Japanese porcelain.

•In the mid 18th century, European floral styles introduced.

•In 1750s transparent lead glaze introduced.

•Tended to copy Meissen and Vincennes porcelain designs.

•From 1755-1780 many floral designs produced, often in one colour, like the 'Chantilly sprig' which was then copied by other factories such as Caughley.

Chelsea (1748-1784)

Note: The names of the different periods refer to the different marks used.

Triangle period, 1745-49

•Many based on silver prototypes and 'Blanc de Chine' ware.

•Mainly undecorated.

•Body comparatively thick, slightly chalky with 'glassy' glaze.

Raised Anchor period, 1749-1752

•Shapes still derived from silver, although Meissen influence is still notable.

•Mostly restrained decoration, with either Kakiemon or sparse floral work (often to cover flaws).

•Often difficult to distinguish from the rare, and sought-after 'Girl in a Swing' factory wares.

•Creamy, almost waxy appearance of glaze is virtually indistinguishable from red anchor glaze, apart from the greater opacity of the later body.

Red Anchor Period 1752-1756

•This period is mainly influenced by Meissen.

•Glaze now slightly opaque.

•Paste smoother with few flaws.

•The figures unsurpassed by any other English factory.

•On useful wares, fine flower and botanical painting.

Gold Anchor Period 1757-1769

•Chelsea's rococo period, distinguished by the rich gilding and characteristic mazarine blue.

•Quite florid in style, in comparison to earlier painting.

•Elaborate bocage (technique of building up models with encrusted leaves and flowers) greatly favoured on figures.

Has thick glaze which tends to craze.

Coalport (1796-1926)

•Early blue and white wares very close in style and feeling to Caughley products.

•Note the somewhat clear royal blue tone of the cobalt.

•Produced hard paste porcelain certainly after 1800, before then produced soapstone porcelain; this was quite similar to Caughley but does not have the yellow-brown translucency.

•Early wares heavy, with greyish appearance.

•In this period quite similar to Newhall and Chamberlains.

•The highly decorated Japan wares were of exceptional quality, as are some of the flower painted examples.

•In 1820, a new leadless glaze was invented and they also began to use Billingsley's frit paste.

•Whereas original Welsh plates were thinly potted, Coalport were heavier and less crisp.

•In 1820, Rose also bought moulds from Nantgarw and Swansea and Billingsea came to work at Coalport.

•Best period for the Coalport factory began in 1820 when the factory produced a brilliantly white hard feldspar porcelain, with a high translucency.

•After 1820, CD, CD monogram, C. Dale, Coalbrookdale and Coalport were all marks used.

•In 1840s and 1850s Coalport perfected many fine ground colours: maroon, green and pink.

•These often rivalled Sèvres, especially in the 1850s and 1860s and are close to the Minton examples of this period.

•Coalport also at this time produced Chelsea copies, with fake marks – these are rare and highly sought after.

•The most desirable pieces are those which are signed by the artists working at Coalport.

Davenport (1793-1887)

•The porcelain produced often imitated Derby porcelain as some of the painters were employed at both factories.

•Early porcelain of a hard paste variety.

•Any Davenport marked 'Longport' is quite rare.

•High-quality wares produced, particularly in 19th century.

•On botanical wares if the flowers are named it can add 50 per-cent to the value.

•High-quality Davenport ware is often wrongly classified as Rockingham ware.

•Davenport produced the Imari styles better known on Royal Crown Derby; this is rarer than Derby but not as collectable.

Derby (1750-1848)
18thC Derby

•Some early white jugs incised with the letter D have been attributed to the early Derby factory.

•Early Derby is soft paste and is lighter than Bow and Chelsea.

•Very rare to find crazing on early Derby; the glaze was tight fitting and thinner than Chelsea.

•Glaze often kept away from the bottom edge, or edge was trimmed, hence the term 'dry-edge' (particularly with figures).

•c.1755, three (or more) pieces of clay put on bottom of figure to keep it clear of kiln furniture, giving 'patch' or 'pad' marks – which now have darker appearance.

•Duesbury's early works display quite restrained decoration, with much of the body left plain, in the Meissen style.

•Derby can be regarded as the English Meissen.

•The porcelain of this period has an excellent body, sometimes with faintly bluish appearance.

•1770-84 known as the Chelsea-Derby period.

•1770s saw the introduction of unglazed, white biscuit Derby.

•This points to the move away from the academic Meissen style towards the more fashionable French taste.

•In 1770s leading exponent of the neo-classical style, and comparable to contemporary wares of Champion's Bristol.

•Body of 1770s is frequently of silky appearance and of bluish-white tone.

•780s Derby body very smooth and glaze white. The painting on such pieces was superb, especially landscapes of Jockey Hill and Zachariah Boreman.

•1780s and 1790s noted for exceptional botanical painting by 'Quaker' Pegg and John Brewer.

•Around 1880 the body degenerated, was somewhat thicker and the glaze tended to crackle and allow discoloration.

Liverpool
Samuel Gilbody's Factory c.1754-1761

•The Gilbody group is the rarest of all Liverpool groups.

•An attractive, sometimes blurred greyish underglaze blue.

•Some blurred blue designs were then enamelled in iron red.

•Heavily potted early wares in blue and overglaze iron red can be confused with Bow wares.

•The typical Gilbody glaze is smooth and silky.

Richard Chaffers & Partners c.1754-1765

•Richard Chaffers & Partners had an earthenware factory in Liverpool during the 1740s.

•In 1755 Chaffers engaged Robert Podmore as manager in return for the secret 'of making earthenware in imitation of or to resemble china ware'.

- Early phosphatic wares have a greyish body.
- Later steatitic wares are noticeably whiter.
- Potting based on Worcester shapes.

William Ball c.1755-1769
- The factory produced a large variety of shapes.
- Decoration often resembled delft.
- Paste often shows small turning tears. These show up as lighter flecks when held up to the light.
- Polychrome wares are rare and collectable.
- Elaborate rococo sauceboats were a factory speciality.

William Reid c.1755-1761
- Often a crude and semi-opaque body.
- Glaze opacified by the use of tin outside.
- Mainly blue and white.
- Reid became bankrupt in 1761 and his factory was occupied by William Ball.

Philip Christian c.1765-1776
- Philip Christian took over Richard Chaffer's factory upon his death in 1765..
- In 1772 Christian renewed his licence to mine steatite at Predannak, Cornwall.
- In 1776 Philip Christian and Son sold their Interest and ceased manufacturing.

James, John and Seth Pennington c.1769-1799
- The majority of the output was blue and white.
- Some highly collectable ship painted dated jugs and bowls produced in 1770s and 1780s.
- A very dark underglaze blue was used in 1770s and 1780s.
- The glaze is sometimes tinted blue-grey.
- Transfer prints often smudgy in appearance.
- Good-quality pieces are the most valuable.

Wolfe & Co c.1795-1800
- In 1795 Thomas Wolfe and partners took over one of the

Pennington family's factories in Liverpool.

•Unlike the other Liverpool factories the vast majority of their output was decorated in polychrome.

•Some of the wares are well-potted and attractively painted.

Longton Hall (1749-60)

•All the wares are rare.

•Earliest pieces are the 'Snowman' figures and some blue and white wares.

•There has been a re-attribution of some Longton wares to West Pans factory started by Wm. Littler in the early 1760s.

•West Pans wares are usually decorated in a crude tone of blue, polychrome decoration is often badly rubbed.

•Some West Pans wares are marked with two crossed Ls with a tail of dots below.

•The figures, in particular, tend to have a rather unattractive stiff, lumpy appearance.

• The porcelain is of the glassy soft-paste type.

•The glaze can tend to have a greenish-grey appearance.

•Pieces often thickly potted.

•Duesbury worked at Longton Hall before going to Derby.

•The 'middle period' of the factory from c.1754-57 saw the best quality porcelain produced.

•Specialized in wares of vegetable form, some of ungainly appearance, unlike the more sophisticated wares of Chelsea.

•Much of the output of the middle period was moulded.

•Two famous painters from the period are the 'castle painter' and the 'trembly rose' painter.

•Sadler's black printed wares are rare and sought after.

Lowestoft (1757-c.1800)

•Soft-paste porcelain using bone ash.

•Damage tends to stain brown.

•Decoration of early wares is well detailed and less stylized than post-1765 porcelain wares.

•No factory mark but many pieces pre-1775 numbered inside footrim or on base if no footrim.

•Numbers are usually between 1 and 11.

•Late period blue and white teabowls and saucers and other common teawares in painted or printed patterns should still be found at reasonable prices, particularly if damaged.

•Coloured wares have been undervalued in recent years and it is still possible to form a collection of extremely interesting pieces without spending a fortune.

•Many collectors are interested in unusual shapes: bottles, inkwells, eggcups, salts, eye baths and so on. Even damaged items can be very collectable but tend to be expensive.

•Lowestoft produced quite a large number of inscribed and dated pieces. These are highly collectable even if damaged. Beware of fakes produced by French factories earlier this century which are hard, rather than soft-paste.

•Early blue and white wares are of great interest to collectors. It is worth consulting a specialist book in order to help identify these pieces correctly as there is a growing tendency to give pieces an optimistically inaccurate early date.

Meissen (1710-present)

•In 1709 J.F. Böttger produced a white hard paste porcelain.

•Wares often decorated by outside decorators (Hausmaler).

•In 1720 kilnmaster Stozel came back to Meissen bringing with him J.G. Herold.

•From 1720-1750 the enamelling on Meissen was unsurpassed – starting with the wares of Lowenfinck – bold, flamboyant Chinoiserie or Japonnaise subjects, often derived from the engravings of Petruschenk, particularly on Augustus Rex wares. J.G. Herold specialized in small elaborate Chinoiserie subjects.

C.F. Herold is best-known noted for his European and Levantine quay scenes.

• Crossed swords factory mark started in 1723.

• Marks, shapes and styles much copied.

• Underside of body on later wares has somewhat greyish chalky appearance.

• In late 1720s glassier, harder-looking paste was introduced, different from the early ivory tones of the Böttger period.

• Finest Meissen figures modelled by J.J. Kändler from 1731.

• Best figures late 1730s and early 1740s – especially the great Commedia dell'Arte figures and groups.

• Other distinguished modellers who often worked in association with Kändler were Paul Reinicke and J.F. Eberlein.

• Early models had been mounted on simple, flat pad bases, whereas from 1750s bases were lightly moulded rococo scrolls.

• Meissen decorations between 1750 and 1814 were among the best ever painted in Europe.

• From the early 19th century the bases of figures are incised with large, cursive numbers and stamped with serif numbers.

Minton (1798-present)
• Factory mainly famous for its bone china.

• Early patterns tend to be similar to those produced by Newhall, Pinxton and Spode.

• Early wares not marked but did often have a pattern number, sometimes with 'N.' or 'No.' in front.

• Minton palette is closest to Pinxton.

• Much pre-1850 Minton is wrongly attributed to other factories especially Pinxton, Rockingham and Coalport.

• The early figures are prone to damage, watch for restoration.

• Very few heavily flower encrusted wares have escaped without some damage over the years.

• Some beautiful ground colours with excellent gilding, Minton had particular success with a turquoise ground.

•As with all factories, top-quality pieces are the most desirable.

•Artists of note include: G. Hancock, J. Bancroft, T. Kirkby, T. Allen, R. Pilsbury. Jesse Smith and A. Boullemier.

Note on marks – 'MINTON' became 'MINTONS' from c.1873.

New Hall (c.1781-c.1835)

•Known as Hollins, Warburton & Co. when it began in 1781, Newhall was the second Staffordshire pottery to make porcelain successfully, Longton Hall being the first.

•Newhall used the Cookworthy method of making a class of porcelain known as hybrid hard-paste.

•Porcelain is a greyish colour to transmitted light and is seldom very crazed.

•Duvivier, who had worked at Derby and Worcester, also painted at Newhall from 1782-1790 – because of the rarity of attributable pieces one wonders if some of his work at Newhall has been wrongly attributed to another factory.

•Very few pre-1790 wares had a pattern number.

•Around 1812 a new bone-china body was introduced and the factory was by this time known as Newhall.

•After 1820 the bone-china wares seemed to lose some quality and the factory closed in 1835.

Pinxton (c.1796-c.1801)

•Factory produced soft-paste porcelain from 1796-1801.

•In the early stages the porcelain, glaze and even designs are similar to Derby.

•The body has good translucency and in comparison with other factories, the palette has a yellow-brown look.

•The glaze is of a fine creamy white with the occasional slight suggestion of blue.

•Well known for its excellent flower painting. Some no doubt are by William Billingsley, a decorator for Derby, who also worked for Swansea and Coalport.

•The factory closed in 1812-13, but it is not certain how much porcelain was produced from 1801 to its closure.

•Pinxton is a rare factory and the yellow-ground wares in particular are sought after.

Plymouth (c.1768-70)

•High proportion of kiln wastage.

•Had a tendency to firing flaws and smokiness as a result of improper technique used in the kiln and imperfections in glaze of the wares.

•Very black underglaze blue.

•Most recognized products are the bell-shaped tankards which are painted with dishevelled birds in the manner of the artist, Monsieur Soqui.

•The shell salt, also known at Worcester, Derby and Bow, most commonly found piece.

•Cookworthy transferred the factory to Bristol c.1770.

Rockingham (1826-1847)

•Potters of the Bramfield family.

•Bone china appears softer than porcelain wares by contemporary porcelain makers.

•Of a smoky ivory/oatmeal colour.

•Factory known for rococo style of decoration, frequently with excellent quality flower painting.

•Tendency to use green, grey and puce.

•Large numbers of erroneous attributions made to the Rockingham factory, especially pieces actually made at Minton and Coalport.

•Pattern numbers over 2,000 are not Rockingham and should always be avoided.

St Cloud (1690s-1766)
• Pieces heavily potted.
• Glaze clear and thick.
• Body has a yellowish tone.
• Until mid-1730s pieces mainly decorated in underglaze blue.
• Also specialized in a variety of pieces which were influenced by the blanc-de-Chine wares.
• After mid-1730s polychrome wares produced.

Samson Edmie Et Cie (1850s-1870s)
• Produced copies of Chinese, German and English porcelain, French faience, Dutch Delft, and, in addition, some wares of the Strasbourg factory.
• Their fakes of Meissen and Chinese porcelain are excellent.
• Their English soft-paste porcelain fakes are easier to detect, as they used a Continental hard-paste body.
• Samson claims that all wares have an 'S' contained within the mark. However this mark can be easily removed by the unscrupulous dealer or collector.
• More pieces have been attributed to Samson than they could possibly have made.

Sèvres (1756-present)
• In early days copied Meissen and influenced by Kakiemon.
• Most decoration of these early years has a somewhat tentative appearance and few pieces show the sharpness of German makers of this period.
• The vases and other hollow wares including ice pails and flower holders epitomized the rococo style at court.
• Sèvres managed to discover the secret of hard paste porcelain at the same time as Cookworthy at Plymouth in 1768.
• 'Jewelled porcelain' was introduced in 1773, using a technique of fusing enamels over gilt or silver foil.

•The most sought-after and valuable ground colour is the yellow ('Jaune jonquille').

•Factory also noted for clock cases, small sets for tea, coffee and chocolate, and boxes.

Swansea Porcelain (1813-22)

•Superb translucent body, excellent glaze.

•In many ways one of the best porcelain bodies produced in the British Isles.

•Also noted for delicacy of flower painting, usually attributed to Billingsley although much was done by other decorators including Pollard and Morris.

•A close study of a marked piece will give one an idea of Billingsley's work, but unless actually signed by him pieces should be marked 'possibly by Billingsley'.

On pieces moulded with the floral cartouches the moulding can be detected on the other side of the rim, unlike the heavier Coalport wares which later utilized the same moulds.

•Especially notable are figure and bird paintings by T. Baxter.

•Swansea mark often faked, particularly on French porcelain at the end of the 19thcentury and beginning of the 20th century.

•In 1816 Billingsley left to start up again at Nantgarw.

•Many pieces decorated in London.

Vienna (1718-1864)

•The body of Du Paquier wares has a distinctive smoky tone.

•Decoration tends to cover much of the body and can be more elaborate then Meissen.

•Extensive use of trellis work or 'gitterwerk'.

•The style of this period was 'baroque', with scrollwork and lattice-like gilding.

•Plain bases were used from the mid-1760s and figure modelling was undertaken by J.J. Niedermayer from 1747-84.

Vincennes (1738-56)
• Early production was generally of indifferent quality.
• Inferior to the productions of St. Cloud and Mennecy.
• Towards end of 1740s introduced coloured grounds.
• 1750s lightly tooled gilding used to heighten reserve panels.
• Coloured grounds: 'Bleu' from the late 1740s; 'Blue celeste' from 1752; 'Jaune jonquille' from 1753; and 'Rose pompadour' from 1757.

Worcester (1751-present)
• c.1751-53 a short experimental period. Sometimes difficult to differentiate between Lund's Bristol and Worcester.
• Both blue and white and 'famille verte' polychrome wares.
• c.1752-54 some wares marked with an incised cross or line.
• c.1755-60 some finely painted and potted wares produced.
• Painters marks resembling Chinese letters appear on base.
• The underglaze blue is well controlled and of a pale colour.
• Polychrome decoration is crisp and clean.
• Almost all patterns are based on Chinese prototypes.
• Transfer printed wares appear c.1754.
• From 1760-1776 a consistently high standard of potting and decorating, though lacking spontaneity of earlier wares.
• Most blue and white pieces now marked with a crescent.
• Often difficult to differentiate from Caughley where open crescent mark also used.

Worcester Porcelain Dates
1751-1783 First Period
1751-1774 'Dr Wall' Period
1776-1792 Davis/Flight Period
1783-1792 Flight Period
1792-1804 Flight and Barr Period
1804-1813 Barr, Flight
1813-1840 Flight, Barr

1788-1840 Chamberlain-Worcester
1840-1852 Chamberlain and Company
1852-1862 Kerr and Binns (W.H. Kerr & Co.)
1862- Worcester Royal Porcelain Company

Oriental Wares

Although Chinese porcelain dates back to the 10th century AD, the pieces you are more likely to come across will be from the Ming (1368-1644) and Qing (1644-1916) dynasties. Marks should be viewed with some caution, as the Chinese often added early Ming marks to pieces made in the Qing period as a mark of veneration for their ancestors. These pieces can be 'in the style of' the earlier period, but not always.

Oriental Porcelain

Good pieces with a hairline crack or small chip can be reduced in value by up to two thirds.

•The rarest pieces, particularly those not made for export, fetch by far the highest prices.

•To distinguish between Ming and Qing you must understand the technical rather than decorative differences between the two: many designs and patterns are common to both.

•Most Ming is more heavily and unevenly glazed, and displays a bluish or greenish tint. Runs and dribbles of glaze can often be detected. Most Qing wares will be found covered in a glaze of uniform thickness.

•Particularly characteristic is the pure white appearance achieved by the Kangxi potters who coated vessels in a thin and even wash.

•However, reigns of Yongzheng and Qianlong did see some pieces deliberately covered in a thick glaze in order to emulate the early 15th-century porcelains.

•The footrims on Ming are generally knife-pared.

METAL WARES

In Britain, all silver wares, with a few minor exceptions, carry 'Hall' or 'Town' marks, which provide precise information on the origin, quality and date of a piece. In Europe and North America marks have never been systemized in this manner, and therefore are not always a reliable method of identification and dating, although they can provide useful clues.

British Silver Marks

There are usually four, but sometimes five or more marks on each piece of silver (illustrated below).

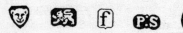

1. The specific Hall or Town mark. These are different for each assay office, and variations occur over the years.

2. Standard or quality mark. All English assay offices show a lion walking to the left (passant) to indicate Sterling quality. Between 1697 and 1719 the silver standard was raised and the existing Hall mark was replaced by Britannia, and the Lion passant by a Lion's Head in profile (illustrated below). When the lower standard was restored in 1719, the original marks were

revived. However, the Britannia marks are permitted on silver that reaches the higher standard. In Scotland, the Edinburgh standard mark is a thistle (used since 1759) (illustrated below). In Glasgow the standard mark is a Lion Rampant (with a thistle since 1914). The Irish Republic has no standard mark, but uses a crowned harp instead.

3. Annual Date Letter. Each assay office allocates its own specific letter, enclosed in a shield, for each year. An alphabetical sequence is normally followed (although J is often omitted).

4. Maker's mark or initial.

5. Sovereign's Head (illustrated below). Appears on pieces between 1784 and 1890, showing duty levied on silver and gold was paid.

6. Jubilee Mark. Commemorates King George V's Silver Jubilee, on article assayed between 1933 and 1936.

7. Leopard's Head. London's Hall mark was sometimes also used as an additional mark by provincial assay offices (except Birmingham and Sheffield).

8. Foreign Silver. From 1843 imported silver articles of the required standard were marked with the letter F. Nowadays each assay office has its own symbol that is applied to all silver articles of foreign origin.

9. Coronation Mark. Shows crowned head of Elizabeth II facing right. Its use was voluntary and restricted to 1952-4. It is important to note that early silver marks are far from uniform, because the punches were hand-made. Hall marks should never be used as a sole guarantee of authenticity, as they have often been faked.

Continental Silver Marks

The number and variation of continental silver marks is so vast, you should refer to the many specialist publications on the subject that are available.

Silver Wares

Fashions come and go, but quality pieces retain their value.

•The best pieces have no damage or alteration, retain their original decoration and carry a full set of marks correctly grouped and spaced.

•Patina should be glowing and unblemished. Breaks in patination are a sure sign of repair or alteration.

•Avoid pieces that have been cleaned with harsh chemicals and have an over-white appearance.

•Poor patina may indicate the use of substandard metal, or that the piece is an electroplate copy or fake.

•Marks should follow the shape of a piece: i.e., arranged in a circle on a round-bottomed piece, and in a line on a square-bottomed one. Each piece of a multipart should have its own set of silver marks.

•All legitimate repairs must be separately marked.

•Repairs reduce the value of a piece.

•Watch out for patched-on Hallmarks. Usually junction lines are visible on a tarnished piece when it is breathed on. Alternatively, examine it under magnification.

•Patched on Hallmarks can be an attempt to deceive. However, between 1719 and 1759 and 1784 and 1790 marks were sometimes taken from a small object and patched on to a more substantial piece to avoid duty. Patination can be a helpful guide to distinguish two forms.

•British pieces made to commission, or in a place remote from an assay office, may not carry assay marks. This doesn't necessarily reduce their value.

•If heraldic arms are in their original state and contemporary with the piece they add value and are a useful guide to dating and provenance. Check with a strong magnifying glass for any re-engraving – a second, sharp line will be seen within the lines of the original decoration.

•Erased or replaced armorials can detract from value. Look for signs of a patch, although this may be difficult to detect if the joins form part of the decoration.

•The areas most susceptible to damage are the joints at handles, spouts, feet and rims. Also check for pin-prick holes where the silver has thinned through handling.

•Beware of marriages. These can be skilfully executed and take a variety of forms. Common examples include a genuinely old Hallmarked base or handle married to a later piece, or apostle finials to other cutlery stems.

Sheffield Plate

The process of fusing a thin sheet of silver to a thicker one of copper dates from the 1740s. British Plate is often confused with Sheffield Plate, and was patented in 1836. Because it was cheaper to produce (the 'German Silver' was only a silver-coloured alloy), tougher and had no reddish copper base to show through when worn, it effectively ended Sheffield Plate production in the 1840s. It was itself superseded by cheaper electro-plating later in the century.

•Sheared edges with metal plating on one side only, revealing a copper edge, indicate Sheffield Plate c.1745-1760.

•Single lapped edges, concealing the copper, are c.1760-1790. Beading was simple and punched in.

•Double lapped edges, in which silvered copper ribbons were soldered to the edges to lap over on to copper undersides, are c1770-1810. They are often difficult to detect. Beading, reeding and gadrooning were in common use at this time.

•Silver lapped edges, in which both sides of the copper sheet were silver-plated and U-shaped silver wire was used to conceal any copper revealed by shearing, are c.1775-1815 – the joins are almost invisible. From 1800, shells, dolphins and oak leaves were used as decoration.

• After 1815, ornamentation was much more elaborate, with vine leaves, flowers and various classical motifs.

• No marks were permitted before 1784. Individual maker's marks (registered with the assay office) appear, after that date, but many pieces remain unmarked.

• Registration of marks ceased in 1835.

• From 1820-1835, fine quality Sheffield Plate could carry a crown mark to distinguish it from lightly silvered imported wares. The proportions of silver and copper were also sometimes stamped on for the same reasons.

• Simulated silver Hallmarks (normally five) start to appear on pieces after c.1835.

• On hollow ware, a useful test to distinguish between Sheffield Plate and electro-plated is to look for a seam – the latter completely covers the piece.

• The words 'Sheffield Plated' indicate a piece is electro-plated and not genuine Sheffield Plate.

• Hollow forms, such as candlesticks, were made in two pieces until the 1830s, so a piece of Sheffield Plate without seams can not be earlier than this.

Pewter

It is relatively easy to distinguish between period and reproduction pewter pieces because up until c1826 the Pewterer's Company laid down stringent standards: size and weight was controlled, marks were used to designate the fineness of the alloy, and makers were required to stamp pieces with their individual touch-marks. Reproductions made from the 1920s onwards rarely comply with these standards.

There are many hundreds of makers' touch marks, and you should refer to a specialist book on pewter to aid you with identification. However, it is important to note that a mark is in itself not a guarantee of date or quality. Fakers often used genuine marks, although these were not always correctly placed. You should be suspicious of sharp edges, where the fake die has been struck too deeply. Also remember that genuine old pewter quite frequently carried no marks at all. This makes it all the more important to gain a feel for period, style and authentic patina.

•Owner's marks, crests and coats of arms enhance value, especially if they confirm provenance.

•Most flatware made in Britain and the United States was hammered. Later reproductions often do not have this extremely desirable feature.

•The best tankards, spoons and flatware were made of leadless hard or plate pewter, and marked.

•Plate pewter and Britannia metal are whiter than inferior lay or trifle pewter, and each has a characteristic ring when struck. Britannia can be mistaken for silver, but never recovers its sheen if allowed to oxidise. Consequently, pieces in original condition are rare and valuable.

•Period pewter is better finished than reproduction – particularly the seams and edges. The latter should be polished, not sharp. Undersides should have concentric rings from lathe turning – many reproductions or later pieces were made from sheet metal and not cast in the traditional manner.

•Check that wear is consistent with use: edges should be soft, hinges worn and knife cuts explicable. The characteristic patina of pewter develops after approximately 50 years and simulated patina on modern copies dulls the surface but does not have the same glow.

•Many Art Nouveau pieces, particularly British and German, show high standards of craftsmanship. Notable examples include Liberty's Tudric range, decorated with Celtic motifs, and pieces by the German Engelbert Kayser (1840-1911).

•The most faked objects are the higher value ones.

CLOCKS AND BAROMETERS

The best prices are paid for clocks in original condition that still work – restoration is very expensive and never regains the full original value.

•Most clocks made after 1698 carry the maker's or retailer's name; if the face is silver it may also carry the maker's marks. Both provide important clues to the origin and value of a piece.

•Watch out for maker's names that have been added to an unsigned clock, or engraved over an erased signature, to enhance the value. These can be difficult to detect and familiarity with a maker's work is necessary to judge whether the quality and style is right for the name.

•On a metal face look for hammer marks on the back, or signs of thinning where the metal was beaten forward to erase an original name.

•Faces should show appropriate signs of age: painted dials should show crazing; wooden faces should have cracks; metal faces should be partly oxidised – if the dial has been cleaned, check the reverse.

•Be wary of a face that seems too elaborate for the case and chapter ring of the clock.

•Check the back of the dial for blocked holes – usually an indication of a marriage between an unrelated dial and movement; where the pillars and winding holes do not match, new ones have been drilled and the originals filled.

•They can also indicate the marriage of a chapter ring (which shows the hour and minute divisions on the dial of a clock) and dial plate. Check the correct feet are securely placed in their original holes and that the decoration of the two parts is compatible and correct.

•Some holes are filled legitimately – where the maker has made a mistake or a worn post has been removed.

•Replacement of hands does not diminish value, provided they are compatible in style and quality with the face.
•Check the bell is original and not cracked. The signs are a clear sound and resonance and a silvery colour. Modern bells have a coarser ring.

Long (Tall) Case Clocks

Check the movement and case belong to each other by examining the block on which the movement sits for redundant holes – these indicate replacement of the clock's original movement.
•If the block is later than the case the original may have been broken and been replaced. Alternatively, it could be a marriage between two clocks of different periods.
•Check the hood is a good fit around the face. It should disguise the edges of the dial, without masking any decoration..
•A second set of marks shows the block supporting the movement has been moved up or down. This indicates a marriage between parts from two different clocks.
•Scrape marks should match the pendulum weight's position.

Wall and Lantern Clocks

Many 19th-century copies and modern fakes exist. Patina and oxidisation, symmetrical engraving on the centre dial and clear resonance of the bell help indicate a genuine piece.
•The characteristic pierced fretwork crown on a lantern clock should fit well into the original feet holes. If not, it has been replaced; sometimes because of damage to the original, but occasionally with a crown bearing the signature of a maker to enhance value.

Acts of Parliament Clocks

Modern copies are generally unsophisticated and are easily detected as the wood looks too new.

Dial Clocks

Avoid 19th-century versions with painted dials in favour of earlier wood, brass or silvered dials, but check for filled holes indicative of an earlier dial added to a later movement.

Skeleton Clocks

Many are made from disparate parts. Originals have delicate, finely pierced wheels with at least four spokes.
• The size and shape of the glass dome, through which you can see the parts, should be in proportion to the clock. The base should be marble or contemporary wood.

Carriage Clocks

Mass-produced from 1850 onwards.
• The face should be enamel and smooth; not thin and corrugated. Modern faces are white, with black numerals.
• A serial number of more than five digits is modern.
• Side glasses were sometimes replaced by painted porcelain or solid gilt panels, which will be different in colour to the case.
• It is impossible to convert from petite to grande sonnerie mode, though many clocks have been modified in the attempt. Only an original grande sonneries carriage is capable of striking in this mode for seven days without rewinding.

Barometers

Early barometers (which date from the late 17th century) should show correct patination to the wood, a greeny-brown oxidisation to the metal (not the black of modern chemical patination) and mellow gold colour to the gilding.
• Barometers normally bear the maker's mark, sometimes accompanied by a date and/or recognition number.
• Marine and other special types of barometer are worth more than domestic versions, expecially in good condition.

GLASS

Fashions dictates price as much as age and intrinsic quality. For example, much Roman glass and 18th-century Continental glass is relatively inexpensive, while good art glass, such as Tiffany and Lalique, and etched/engraved 18th-century English glass is far more sought after and can command premium prices.

Virtually all types of glass have been copied and reproduced during the 19th and 20th centuries (in the United States sometimes using the original moulds). Consequently, to recognise originals you have to handle glass frequently to become familiar with period shapes, decoration and techniques. However, you should note the following:

• The earliest lead glass has a greenish tinge and it becomes progressively more transparent and colourless over a long time – approximately 150 years.

• Lead glass has a pleasing ring when tapped with a fingernail (some thicker versions may not display this characteristic).

• Old lead glass has a bluish tinge under ultra-violet light. Modern lead glass looks yellow to brown under ultra-violet light. However, oxidated pieces will not respond to this test.

• Coloured glass is unlikely to be old. Until c.1860 its use was mainly restricted to bottles, decanters and tumblers.

• The presence of bubbles is no indication of age. However, most glass with bubbles is 20th century.

• Most genuine 18th-century tableware has a pontil mark (the mark made by the pontil rod, with which the glass is removed from the blowpipe) on the base. If it has been ground off there may be a polished circle where it was removed. However, the presence of a pontil mark is no guarantee of age.

• Old glass may show signs of vertical creases in the bowl, and a nick or lump in the rim where surplus glass was sheared off. Lack of these marks is cause for suspicion.

ART NOUVEAU AND ART DECO

Condition is paramount to the value of Art Nouveau and Art Deco pieces. Even the slightest damage will reduce the value substantially. However, many pieces were produced in quantity and survive in perfect condition.

•The popularity of Art Nouveau and Art Deco has resulted in numerous copies and reproductions. The golden rule is: "Let the buyer beware". However, the following are worth noting:

•Numerous fakes, often cast in the original moulds, have been made of bronze and ivory pieces produced in the 1920s and '30s, particularly in Vienna and Paris. Look for crudely carved ivory hands and feet and poor joins between ivory and bronze.

•Signatures on glass pieces are often forged. It is sensible to ask for documentary support for the provenance of a piece.

•There are numerous modern copies of original lamps, particularly Tiffany and designs produced at the factories of Steuben, Quezal and Brooklyn J Hardel. However, they lack the quality and finish of the originals.

RUGS AND CARPETS

You should refer to specialist publications that detail the numerous rug makers and rug making regions around the world, as ascertaining make and date with absolute certainty can be difficult. However, the following points are worth noting for the purposes of identification:

•The older the rug, the greater its investment potential.

•Almost as important are richness of colour, how interesting the design is, together with the degree of age and patination.

•The best rugs, and the ones that acquire the highest prices, are made by the tribal people of Asia Minor. Top of the scale are fine silk rugs from Persia and Turkey. Quality wool rugs from Persia and the Caucasus also command high prices. More recent Chinese, Indian and Pakistani rugs, usually of wool, are far less valuable.

•Hand-made rugs have the pattern visible on the back as well as the surface. Part the pile and look for rows of knots at the base of the tuft. Absence of either indicates a machine-made rug, which is of much less interest to collectors.

•Synthetically dyed rugs, introduced in the 1920s, are often garish and lack strength. Chemical dyes come off on a white handkerchief wetted with saliva, and have an unpleasant smell. Some vegetable dyes also leave a stain, but this is slight.

•The back of an old rug will have a polished appearance and the knots will be flattened.

•The foundation threads at the base of the pile should be yellowish-grey with age, even if the rug has been cleaned.

•Check tufts with a magnifying glass: in old rugs the colour should shade gradually from deep at the base to pale at the tip. Three distinct bands of colour indicate artificial ageing.

•Never buy a rug that has been attacked by mildew. The signs are light-coloured patches on the back and rotten fibres which snap when the rug is folded or twisted.

•Check for holes and wear by holding up to the light. Repairs can be effected, but are costly. However, if executed skilfully with correctly matching colours using vegetable dyes, they will not substantially affect the value of the rug of carpet.

•Repairs can be detected with the palm of the hand as raised or uneven areas of pile.

•Many rugs have had worn areas removed. Check the pattern is contained within the frame and does not run beyond the edge of the carpet. Also check the end borders match the side ones and have not been replaced.

•It is better to buy a rug with a replaced fringe than one in which the fringe has been removed, or where a new fringe has been made by simply fraying the edges of the rug.

•Dates (in arabic characters) woven into the rug are helpful, but can be misleading. Some weavers copied earlier rugs, together with their dates.

•Dates may have been altered to increase the apparent age – check carefully for signs of new weaving, especially around the second numeral.

ARMS AND ARMOUR

Armour

This is not an area for the novice. Genuine full suits are very rare and extremely expensive. Even reproductions, such as those made in the 19th century in Germany, France and Spain, are sought after and relatively valuable. Marriages of originally unrelated items are common. Condition, general wear and patina are all important factors in determining authenticity and value. You should refer to specialist books on the subject. However, the following points are worth noting:

•Helmets are often marriages, and you should check joints and hinges to ensure they are original.

•Genuine 17th-century armour often has an armourer's mark plus small dents from a pistol ball fired at close rangto 'prove' the strength of the breastplate. However, do not rely on these marks as they are sometimes faked.

•Modern reproductions have probably been gas-welded. This can produce burn marks on the surface.

•Beware of inferior Chinese armour being passed off as something more valuable.

•Beware of crude bazaar copies of genuine Indian and Middle Eastern coloured armour.

•Be careful not to damage or remove any marks which may be concealed beneath rust.

Edged Weapons

Very few genuinely old swords have their original scabbards. Made of thin wood, leather or velvet, they quickly deteriorated.

•Hundreds of thousands of Japanese swords were mass-produced during the Second World War. These should not be confused with genuinely old, and highly valuable examples.

•Numerous Middle Eastern and Indian swords were produced in the 20th century.

•On early swords, spurious maker's marks have often been added, while later military swords have faked presentation inscriptions etched or engraved to give false connections with famous personalities or memorable events (such as The Charge of the Light Brigade).

•Fake etching has a different depth to the original blade etching, and there will be a difference in background colour.

•Fine lines should be filled with the dirt and grease accumulated over time, and there should be no suspiciously bright edges to the weapon.

•A great number of mass-produced swords and daggers have been exported from India during the past 20 years. These are roughly forged, of inferior quality and relatively valueless.

General Militaria

•Excellent reproductions of old powder flasks are in circulation, many aged and faked to appear original. To check, look for traces of new solder and bright metal.

•Numerous fake badges, insignia and buttons are in circulation. They tend to be lighter than originals, and the badges tend to have a waxy feel.

Firearms

•Flintlocks vary greatly in quality and price. Authenticated pistols by some of the most well-known makers command high prices. Consequently, faking is not unknown. Check for fresh looking file or cut marks.

•If suspicious, ask for the lock-plate to be removed: evidence of tampering may lie behind it.

•Legitimate repairs to the seat or main spring are acceptable, provided they are declared and reflected in the price.

•Many English pieces have a proofmark on the barrel. Size, shape and design reveal the year it was stamped. However, sometimes marked barrels were married to foreign stocks and furniture, either at the time or later on. Consequently, marks are only clues. (Note that America had no comparable system.)

•Maker's names, usually engraved on the lock plate, are also clues. (You should refer to a specialist publication on firearms for a comprehensive list of leading makers.)

•If an unmarked flintlock seems very cheap it may be from the Middle or Far East.

•The parts of a Colt revolver were individually numbered, and those with matching numbers are highly desirable. If the numbers do not match it may be replaced. However, check to see if any attempt has been made to change the numbers.

•Numerous late 19th-century, poorish quality Colts, originally made for the Middle Eastern market, are in circulation. These are often sold as 'genuine' standard 'Army', 'Navy' or 'Pocket' Colts. They may also have been doctored to conceal their origin and fake highly priced models. So, be careful to check all serial numbers, ramrods, cylinders and barrel lengths, as these may have been altered.

•If a weapon feels top-heavy and uncomfortable in the firing position, be suspicious, particularly if it is highly priced.

•If there is rusting, check if it is consistent over the barrel, furniture and lock – it should be.

•Cased sets of pistols should be carefully checked to confirm all items belong together, and that some are not later additions.

DOLLS, TEDDY BEARS AND TOYS

You should refer to specialist publications on the subject, but also note the following:

•Most collectors are interested in dolls made before the First World War. Original condition is important – clothes should be retained and the dolls should never be repainted.

•Automata are particularly valuable. Some have porcelain marks which aid dating.

•Teddy bears are highly collectable, particularly those by Steiff, and especially those with a working growl.

•Reproductions, particularly of dolls, abound. Hair and styles of clothing are important clues to period – no doll with machine-stitched clothes can be earlier than the sewing machine (invented 1850). Nylon hair also indicates a modern copy.

CHAPTER FOUR

HOW TO BUY

£

Having learnt as much as you can about antiques, collectables and their prices from books and magazines, looking at and handling them, talking to experts, and sitting in on auctions, you will reach the point where you feel sufficiently confident to begin buying them. Whether you intend to purchase antiques purely for the pleasure of owning or collecting them, as a long-term investment, or as a part- or full-time business, you will definitely need to know the best places to buy, and how to buy for the best possible price.

The Attic

The first place you should look – your own home – doesn't actually involve you in buying. Moreover, it might surprise many people to know that some of the leading antiques dealers in the country started out this way. If you recognise something of value up in the attic, out in the garage, or in the living room, and you go on to sell it, everything you make is pure profit – there's no overhead or purchase price, and all or most of the money can be invested in acquiring new pieces.

Not so long ago one couple found a dented, copper-bodied jug in their attic. Embellished with various motifs, applied in silver and including three fish-in-fronds, a lobster, two dragonflies and a frog, it was by Tiffany & Co., and made £11,000 at auction; the money getting the couple off to a flying start for future buying and selling.

Not everyone can be so lucky, but there are plenty of other places to look, which are described below.

Friends

However fortunate you are, it is unlikely that you will find among your possessions a sufficient number of items to take, for example, a stall at a local antiques fair. So, at some point you'll have to start looking beyond your own front door. Again, a number of dealers I know started out by either buying pieces from friends, or selling on their behalf for a commission. The latter can be an attractive option, particularly if you are short of capital. Chapter Six (see pages 132-149) covers the ins-and-outs of selling antiques, but for now I would simply say that friendships are more important than money. If you offer a friend say £20 for something in the full knowledge that you could sell it on immediately for £300, they are hardly likely to give you a pat on the back and praise to all and sundry your entrepreneurial talents. Be totally up-front with friends: tell them that you're offering to buy the piece for £X because you can sell it for £Y, your overheads (time, travel, auction charges, paying for a stall, shop rent, whatever) are £W and your profit is £Z (which shouldn't be less than 25 per cent of £Y if you are in business and you want it to be profitable). In other words, spell it out that: X = Y-W-Z. This way, everyone knows where they stand, and can take it or leave it (at the end of your gentle persuasions). It also means that your friends are far more likely to want to do business with you again. (They may commission you to buy things for them – again, see Chapter Six.)

Jumble Sales and Charity Shops

Whether you are an amateur or a professional, two places worth looking for antiques and collectables are jumble sales and charity shops. The former (which are advertised in weekly local newspapers) are rarely the source of very valuable pieces. This is because many organisers are sufficiently clued-up nowadays to have anything that they think might be worth more

than a bob or two valued by a trusted local dealer or auctioneer. In other words, by the time the sale is open to the public,
such pieces are long gone.

However, I do know of someone who went to live in the
West Country for a year (her office relocated), and every
Saturday attended one or two local jumble sales specifically to
look for period costume from 1920s and 1930s. By the end of
the year she had accumulated plastic bin liners full of dresses,
skirts, blouses, hats, shoes, fans and costume jewelry, etc.,
most of them bought for less than a couple of pounds each. On
moving back to London, she took a stall at a well-known weekend market, and within a month had sold all of her stock to
fellow stall-holders and members of the public for several thousand pounds. As she was only doing it as a hobby, and
therefore wasn't counting her time spent as an overhead, she
reckoned her profit, even taking into account paying for the
stall, was in the region of 2,000 per cent on the purchase price.
My friend's advice to anyone going to a jumble sale was:

1. Find out when it starts and get there half-an-hour early to be
very near the front of the queue.

2. Take lots of coins and small denomination notes, so that you
waste no time waiting for change if you buy anything.

3. When they open the doors make a quick assessment of the
areas on the tables that are likely to be of interest to you, and
head straight for the first of them.

4. Rummage as quickly and as systematically as you can
through the various piles, pulling out and keeping a firm grip
on anything you want to buy – speed is of the essence.

5. If the price isn't marked ask the assistant and, unless the
item really has been over-priced (which is very unlikely at a
jumble sale), hand over the exact money and move rapidly on
to the next area.

6. There will almost certainly be other people interested in the

same items as you. To make sure you get them you may have to be rather determined. Some jumble sales are a bit like a basketball match – it's supposed to be a non-contact sport, but isn't. The worst offenders, believe it or not, tend to be diminutive little old ladies, with sharp and surprisingly hard elbows that they're not shy about bringing in to play. Of course, it's all done very subtly, and whether you respond in kind is a matter for you and your conscience.

Charity shops are similar to jumble sales in that the people who run them also tend to get a local dealer or auctioneer in to look at anything that might be particularly valuable before it goes on display. However, it is surprising how often interesting pieces seem to slip through the net. The friend who made the enormous profit on period clothing also always seems to find incredibly good bargains in her local Oxfam shops: Monart glass vases bought for £7.50 each and worth approximately £120 each; Lloyd-loom chairs bought for between £5 and £10 and worth over £40 etc. The plain fact of the matter is she is fairly knowledgeable about quite a wide range of antiques and collectables, and thus knows what she's looking for. Equally, she has developed an instinct or an 'eye' for a bargain.

Junk Shops

Having an 'eye' for a bargain also affords you the chance of picking up bargains from junk shops. Most of them buy their stock in job-lots from house clearance sales (usually arranged by solicitors or members of the family after the owner has died). While you will be unlikely to come across many authentic antiques in junk shops, they can be a very good source for early 20th-century furniture and a wide range of collectables – tins, cigarette cards, ceramics, glasses etc.

Owners tend to have a rather limited knowledge of antiques. Consequently, if you spot something, the trick is to buy it without alerting them to its true value. Years ago, a friend spotted a reasonably rare 1950s Macgregor driver among a motley collection of old golf clubs, in a junk shop in Exeter. The owner wanted £7 for the lot (including a tatty old canvas golf bag). The bag and all the other clubs were virtually worthless, but rather than saying he was only interested in the driver – which might have raised suspicions – my friend bought the lot without quibbling. He sold on the driver to a collector for £70 and gave the other clubs to a charity shop.

Car Boot Sales

In recent years there have been numerous stories of people who know what they're looking for picking up some incredible bargains at car boot sales (also known as boot fairs). Examples include a 400-year-old German beer stein made of buff-coloured stoneware at Sieburg in the Rhineland. Bought for only £2, its identity was confirmed at Holloway's of Banbury, and it subsequently made £530 at auction. Similarly, four early Doulton 'Bunnykins' figures, which cost a Cheltenham family £4.60 at a boot fair, sold for £3,600 (double the pre-sale estimate) at Sotheby's in Sussex, while a pair of late 17th-century Imari models of cockerels found at a boot sale in Liverpool were eventually bought by a Japanese dealer based in London for £7,500. Perhaps the best example of someone capitalizing on their knowledge was, however, the student of ceramics who recognized the Hans Cooper seal on the back of a shallow stoneware dish at a sale in Farnborough. He snapped it up for £1.50 and sold it at Christie's for £19,000.

It is stories like these that have contributed to the ever-increasing appeal of car boot sales. Usually held in farmers' fields, school play grounds or car parks, they are advertised in local papers, the classified columns of magazines, or on notices pinned to trees or lamp posts in the area. Some are regular events held throughout the year, usually on a Saturday or Sunday, while others are one-offs. You can buy or sell anything at a boot sale, but from the buyer's point of view they can be an inexpensive source of collectables. However, you must be prepared to sift through piles of junk to find these often elusive treasures. Over the years I've bought quite a few nice pieces from boot fairs, and would give the following tips to anyone going along to buy:

1. Arrive early if you want to snap up the bargains before anyone else does.

2. In the winter take a torch along with you. The light can be poor early in the morning or late in the afternoon, and you need to be able to closely inspect items before you part with any of your cash.

3. Take plenty of coins and small denomination notes. There's nothing more infuriating than finding something and having to wait ages to pay for it until the seller finds some change. Don't expect the vendor to take a cheque or credit card.

4. Ask the price, if it isn't already marked, and be prepared to haggle – something is worth only what someone is willing to pay for it on the day.

Adverts

It is worth scouring through the private 'For Sale' ads in local newspapers. For example, I once rang up to enquire about what was described as 'a lovely old set of dining chairs and matching extendible table. Good condition. £70 o.n.o.'. Having heard a fuller description from the owner over the telephone, I expressed an interest and made an appointment. On arrival I was confronted with a rather badly made, mahogany veneered table, from the early 1950s. The chairs, however, were another matter: a set of eight (including two carvers) high-quality Victorian Chippendale, recovered in a ghastly pink draylon. I paid the asking price, re-sold the table (also through a local ad.) for £20 and put the chairs into a local auction where, despite the draylon, they fetched £1,200.

I'd give this advice about buying from a private advert:

1. Having read the advertisement, telephone to find out as much as you can about the piece as possible before you go and see it – i.e. How big is it?, What condition is it in?, Is the price negotiable?, etc.

2. Ask for the vendor's name, address and telephone number.

3. Try to take someone, such as a friend or another member of the family, along with you. If you have to go alone, leave the details of where you're going, and what time you expect to be back with someone – you can't be too careful nowadays.

4. Examine the piece thoroughly and don't take the vendor's word for its age or authenticity, etc.

5. If you decide to buy it, or leave a deposit, ask for a written receipt, which should include the amount, the date, plus the name and address of the vendor. If the worse came to the worst, and it turned out you were buying stolen goods, the receipt would show that you had bought in good faith.

Auctions

Auctions provide one of the most exciting ways of buying antiques and collectables. I've been buying at auction for many years now, but I still get a tremendous buzz from them: the exhilaration of attending the preview and finding something I really want; the tension of walking around and seeing other people pick up 'my' piece and, horror of horrors, mark it down in their catalogue; the anxiety of working out my price limit the night before and wondering if it will be high enough; the mounting stress as the auctioneer gets closer and closer to 'my' lot – heart thudding and palms sweating as the bidding begins; the thrill of securing the prize (especially if I've had to pay less than I was prepared to); or the disappointment of losing it to a higher bid – it's not surprising that many people find auctions addictive.

From the point of view of making money out of antiques, auctions offer the private buyer the opportunity to compete with the trade on equal terms. The statistical fact that most auction lots are bought by the trade, and that members of the trade hardly ever pay 'over the odds' to secure a lot – after all, they have a business to run – means that private buyers can purchase at what you might call 'wholesale' prices.

In terms of the quality of antiques for sale there are various types, or levels, of auctions. At the top of the tree are the big London salerooms of famous firms such as Sotheby's, Christie's, Bonham's and Phillips. These account for the majority of high-quality and expensive antiques and collectables. They all hold regular sales devoted to particular items, such as silver once a fortnight, carpets once a month, treen once a year. Most of the people attending these sales are either dealers or serious collectors, and many lots go to faces known to the auctioneer.

The leading auction houses also have smaller provincial branches, which hold a greater number of general sales. The antiques that pass through them tend to be of a lesser quality than those in the London salerooms, although many fine quality pieces do come up. In addition, there is a country-wide network of independent local auctioneers. Their sales, attended by private and casual buyers and dealers, in roughly equal proportion, are usually general rather than specialized. And the quality of items for sale varies enormously – from rather nice pieces, through bric-a-brac, to old fridges and second-hand 'junk'.

Regardless of the type of auction, the large turnover of items means that there is always the possibility of uncovering what the trade describes as a 'sleeper' – an undiscovered treasure. However, while fine-quality pieces are picked up in the

London salerooms for bargain prices by knowledgeable buyers, the collective expertise of those in attendance means the description 'bargain' has to be qualified.

For example, if I pick up a mid-Georgian mahogany bachelor's chest for £3,000, I might consider it a bargain if I saw a similar piece in a Bond Street showroom for twice that amount. However, if I wanted to sell it on for £6,000, I would either have to have a Bond Street showroom myself, or a number of clients/collectors on my books or among my acquaintances who were prepared to pay that sort of asking price. It would be no good putting the piece straight back into another London auction. In other words, how you define a bargain, or a good price, depends partly on whether you want to keep it or sell it, and, if the latter, who you can sell it to (see Chapter Six, How to Sell, pages 132-150).

The plain fact of the matter is, unless you are a well-established dealer, or a professional collector who also deals, you are unlikely to make money out of antiques in the short term by buying from the London salerooms. Provincial and suburban auctions, however, provide many more opportunities for discovering real bargains, and therefore, if you wish to capitalize on it, short-term financial gain.

For example, some years ago I popped into a sale in Leominster, where I noticed a mixed lot of eight 19th-century Chinese plates, on top of which was a small Worcester tea cup, hand-painted with the Tambourine Pattern and made in the late 1750s. Unfortunately, it was badly damaged, but, as a collector of Worcester, I really liked it and decided to bid a maximum of £130 for the lot. I kept looking round the saleroom to see if there were any other dealers or collectors there who might be interested, but when the auctioneer asked for an opening bid of £30 there was no response. There were no takers for £20 either, so he asked for someone to start him off at £5. There was a bid to my left at £6, then £7 … £8 … £9 … £10 … I raised my catalogue at £11, and absolute silence followed until the auctioneer called 'once … twice … gone to the lady in the middle', accompanied by the sound of the hammer. The lot was mine for £11 – an absolute snip. The eight plates were all good examples of Chinese export ware, and made lovely Christmas presents. As for my cup, well, I still have it and a couple of years later a similar one, also badly damaged, made £500 at auction.

I got my bargain because, first I knew what I was looking at, and second because there were no other dealers or collectors there sufficiently interested in the piece. This happens more than you would think, but it makes sense: there are hundreds of auctions all over the country every week, many of them held on the same day. Dealers and collectors can't be in two places at once, so inevitably you're going to get occasions when there are no other serious rival bidders present.

Of course, it is still possible to pick up tremendous bargains, even if other knowledgeable bidders are present. You just have to know that bit more, or have a 'gut feeling' about something. A wonderful story I heard about five years ago concerned a small-time dealer in Kent who, to save him from the close attentions of the Inland Revenue, we'll call Bill. Attending a local auction preview, he spotted an old book which, even though he didn't know exactly what it was, he knew was the oldest thing he'd ever seen in his life. Sitting in a café and going through the lots with some fellow dealers before the sale, Bill said he would go up to £400 on the book, at which point the others fell about laughing and said he must be mad.

Just before the lot came up, however, a well-known antiquarian book dealer came into the saleroom. This confirmed Bill's suspicions: the book must have been very valuable for the dealer to have attended in person rather than, as was his usual custom, send a representative. Well, the bidding reached £800 before the dealer came in, and he and Bill took it up to £1,250 , with Bill having the final say. The dealer left with the parting shot that he didn't think Bill could even read, while Bill's friends, who had tried to stop him throughout, were virtually on the floor and almost in need of medical attention!

When Bill got the book home, having nearly bankrupted himself, he showed it to his young assistant and said they were both going to take a trip up to London. The reception he received from one of the leading auction houses was initially rather patronizing; a trainee on the counter, having eyed Bill and his assistant up and down, and having given the book only a cursory glance, told him that it was hardly the sort of thing they would be interested in. Bill, however, remained convinced that he was really on to something. Marching out he hailed a cab and told the driver to take him to another leading house, in St James's, where he asked for their top specialist on historic manuscripts and books.

Within seconds of examining the book, the expert's jaw dropped. Bill and his young assistant were ushered into a plush backroom and given tea and cakes, while various other learned-looking individuals inspected the manuscript. After a while, Bill was told that his recent acquisition might be extremely important, and would he mind leaving it with them for a couple of weeks so that further enquiries could be made.

On his return, Bill was told that his book was a 13th-century Atlas of the Universe, of which there were only three other known examples, all of them in museums, and that at auction it would probably fetch in the region of £125,000. Apparently Bill had the 'brass' to suggest that, seeing it was so rare, the auction house ought to reduce their seller's commission, which they did. Bill's book sold for £90,000 – more than a reasonable return on his initial outlay of £1,250!

In many respects Bill broke just about all the rules on buying at auction: he didn't know exactly what he was buying, and he became so determined to get it that he fell prey to 'auction fever' and bid way beyond his pre-set limit. This is an exception that breaks the rule: sometimes if you go with your instinct or 'gut feeling' you can pull off a real coup and make serious money – more often than not, however, you will end up with egg on your face and a depleted bank balance.

At the other end of the spectrum, there have been numerous examples of people furnishing their entire home for less than £200 by buying everything from country auction rooms. Recently, *The Times* recounted the case of a man who had managed to do it for £125 by attending three East Anglian auctions held on the same weekend. Some of the prices he paid may seem incredible, but they are not at all unusual: £2 for a complete bathroom suite; £6 for a dining table; £4 for seven dining chairs; £1 for a wardrobe, and £25 for a sideboard (he obviously got carried away with the bidding on that one!).

The salerooms of a typical country auction are invariably crammed full of all manner of objects, piled haphazardly on tables or stacked against the walls in no particular order. Mirrors, dolls, washstands, tables, ceramics, paintings, jewelry, silver, clocks, chests-of-drawers, chairs, etc., stand side by side or on top of each other. Mixed lots are common. For example, the same East Anglian man picked up a box containing a pair of children's Wellington boots, two dolls, one 12in saucepan, a candelabrum and four tea cups for £1, and another one of assorted kitchenalia, including a dinner plate, a meat dish, knives and forks, a tin opener and a spatula, also for £1. On the other hand, at the same sales a pair of satinwood lyre-end occasional tables fetched £642, and an oak desk made £11,000. In terms of price, the range of items for sale at these sorts of auction is diverse, to say the least. However, while there is no record of the quality of the items this gentleman bought, precedent says that among them there will have been objects that would have cost ten times as much, or more, in an antique shop – in other words, bargains in anyone's book. To maximize your chances of picking up bargains, I recommend you adopt the following approach to every auction:

1. Buy a catalogue: either at the preview or, if they are available, by post in advance. Catalogues vary from the glossy and often fairly expensive illustrated publications produced by the leading auction houses, to typed sheets of paper from smaller, suburban and country auctions. They all, however, list the objects for sale – known as 'lots' – in the sequence in which they will be sold, each lot having its own lot number.

Most catalogues include an estimated price guide for each lot, although at some auctions the estimates are printed on a separate sheet of paper pinned on a wall in the saleroom. It is important to remember that estimates are the price the valuer at the auction house expects the object to fetch, and, as such, are only rough guides. Ultimately, any antique, no matter how rare or valuable, is worth only what two or more people are willing to bid for it. For example, the world record for a teddy bear at auction is £55,000, paid for a 1920 Steiff 'dual plush', or 'bicolour'. This was far in excess of its estimate, and the result of two buyers bidding through agents and giving them no price limit. The new owner was apparently 'gob-smacked' when told what he had spent, which goes to show you should always set yourself a price limit in advance.

2. Attend the sale preview: auction houses usually put the lots on view two days before the sale. You will then be able to examine any pieces in which you are interested at your leisure.

3. Closely examine lots you like: catalogues for important sales include descriptions of the pieces with the valuer's opinion of the date and authenticity of a piece. You should also ask to speak to the specialist in charge of the sale if you want any more information. However, always make up your own mind on matters such as authenticity and price and always carefully inspect for any damage. Professional restoration can be very expensive, and finding a good restorer can be difficult.

4. Don't forget additional costs: when assessing how much you are prepared to pay for something, remember you will have to pay, on top of your bid, a buyer's premium (usually 10 to 15 per cent of the hammer price – the price at which the object is sold in the saleroom), plus V.A.T. on the premium. However, if a lot is being sold on behalf of a company or a V.A.T.-registered person, some auction houses now charge V.A.T. on the bid price itself, although this is always made very clear in advance.

5. Register to bid: at some sales you may have to get a registration number in order to bid. This involves either giving your name, address and telephone number at the reception desk, and/or being issued with a numbered card to hold up should your bid prove successful.

6. Check acceptable methods of payment: if you do not intend to pay by cash, ask in advance whether a cheque or credit card is acceptable. For large sums, some auction houses insist on a banker's reference. Check when you have to settle up too.

7. Leave instructions: if you are unable to attend the sale yourself, you can always leave your bid (the highest price you are prepared to go up to) with the commission clerk or, in smaller auctions, with the auctioneer or one of the porters. They will bid on your behalf. It is usual to tip a helpful porter, but not a clerk or an auctioneer.

8. Get there in plenty of time: some sales last for several hours and if the lots in which you are interested are towards the end you may not want to arrive at the start. At the preview, ask the auction house how many lots they get through in an hour, and work out roughly when your lots will come up. The average is

100 lots per hour. However, some auctioneers, especially at country sales, can get through 130 or more. So, allow a reasonable margin for error – there's nothing more galling, and I've done it myself, than arriving just in time to see the hammer go down on the piece on which you had set your heart.

9. Make sure there's no one else in the room who might bid on your behalf: this may sound silly, but it's not unknown for a dealer or private collector absent-mindedly to instruct more than one agent to bid on his or her behalf; neither of the agents aware of the other's role and bidding against each other.

On a more personal note, one of my most embarrassing experiences occurred a few years ago at Sotheby's, in Bond Street, London. I had gone there to buy some 19th-century Japanese prints, and had a very successful morning: by pure chance there had been two other major sales – one in Paris, one in London – on the same day, so there were very few dealers and collectors at 'my' sale. As a result, I bought about 50 wonderful prints for an average of £8 each. Feeling flushed with success, I walked into a treen sale in one of the other rooms. I'd viewed the lots the day before, and had noticed some very fine wooden bowls. Arriving just in time, and standing at the back of the saleroom, I thought I'd hold back until the others had battled it out. At the appropriate moment I caught the auctioneer's eye and made my bid. 'Mrs Miller', he said, as everyone turned towards me, 'I would be delighted to accept your bid, but I do feel Mr Miller bidding on my left might not be that impressed'.

10. Bid with confidence: people who have never been to an auction before often worry that an ill-timed cough, twitch or sneeze could be mistaken as a bid and land them with an unwanted lot and a hefty bill. This is a myth. In fact, if you are bidding for the first time, especially in a crowded saleroom, it can be quite difficult to attract the auctioneer's attention. Don't be faint-hearted: wave your catalogue or bidding card, or call out if need be. After you have registered your first bid, the auctioneer will probably take any of your subsequent bids on a simple nod. And if he returns to you and you don't want to go any further, a sideways shake of the head should do it. Also, don't worry if the bidding is rising rapidly and the auctioneer appears to be ignoring you. Usually he will only take bids from two people at a time. When one drops out he will look around the room for someone else to join in, and so on ….

Auctioneers invariably start the bidding at a sum just below the lower estimate in the catalogue. If there are no bids at that point, he will ask for an even lower sum and perhaps lower it further until bidding begins. When people wave or nod to him he will call out their bids in regular sums, known as increments. Depending on the value of the piece, the bidding can rise in £5s, £10s, £20s, £50s, £100s, £1,000s, £10,000s or £1,000,000s. When the auctioneer appears to have only one bidder left, he or she will double check to see if anyone else is interested, and then signal the end of the bidding by banging a small hammer (known as a gavel) on the rostrum, and recording the 'knockdown' price and the name or bidding number of the successful bidder.

11. Don't get caught up in 'auction fever': you will have set yourself a price limit either at or just after the preview. However fervent the bidding, my advice is: stick to it (or just possibly go one bid further if you really covet the piece in question). Professional dealers hardly ever go beyond their limit – a figure that they will have worked out beforehand to the nth degree exactly.

Before moving on from buying at auction to buying from dealers, there are two controversial areas associated with auctions that you need to know about. The first is a process whereby the auctioneer bids 'off the wall'. The second concerns the bidding 'controlled' by an 'auction ring'. The former is not only legal, but requisite, while the latter is illegal.

'Off the Wall': An auctioneer represents the seller of a lot, and has a duty to try to ensure the bidding reaches the reserve. The reserve is the lowest price, agreed beforehand between the auction house and the seller, that the lot will be sold for. If there is only one interested bidder in the saleroom, or none at all, the auctioneer must keep the bidding going. He does this by acknowledging fictitious bids from the back or sides of the saleroom (i.e. the walls). Once he reaches the reserve (which is confidential), he will either sell it to the sole bidder in the room or, if there were no real bidders, withdraw the lot.

My advice to anyone who notices that, apart from the wall, they are the sole bidder is to stop bidding, approach the auctioneer after the sale and try to negotiate a price below the reserve. This is known as a private treaty sale. If the seller agrees, you might well have a bargain on your hands.

'The Ring': This is an illegal conspiracy to deflate the prices paid at auction, and is achieved by two or more dealers agreeing in advance not to bid against each other. One of them – the ring leader – bids on behalf of all of them. They then re-auction the lot, or lots, later among themselves – an activity known in the trade as 'the knock out'.

There is no doubt that rings do operate from time to time, although you would be hard-pushed to prove their existence. From the seller's point of view, he should be protected from the ring if the auction house has put a proper reserve on the piece. From the buyer's point of view, there are some people who believe that if a ring is active it is possible for a private buyer to secure a lot at a lower price than otherwise. On the other hand, others believe that a ring, to protect its own interests, will 'run up' the bidding in order to make a private buyer pay over the odds, and thereby discourage him in the future. I have actually seen this happen. However, if you stick to your price limit, a ring will not be able to affect you.

Sticking to your price limit, and knowing what you're bidding for are, of course, the prerequisites of making money from auctions. If we are to believe (I don't) the American writer, Ambrose Brice, in his *Cynics Word Book* (1906), they will also protect you from the auctioneer, whom he describes as: 'the man who proclaims with a hammer that he has just picked a pocket with his tongue'.

Dealers

There is an old saying in the antiques trade that if you know what you're looking for, there's a bargain to be found on every market stall and in every antique shop. I'd go along with this, although, as with auctions, it depends on what you mean by a bargain and why you are buying. For example, if you're looking to sell-on quickly you're unlikely to make a profit on something bought from a top London or provincial dealer, or a stand at an international antiques fair. This is not to say, however, that you wouldn't get your money back. Indeed, many top dealers are usually prepared to buy back a piece for the price you paid for it, or even, if the market price has risen, for more than you paid. There is also the additional advantage of guaranteed authenticity: dealers who are members of either B.A.D.A. or L.A.P.A.D.A. are governed by very strict rules, and if it turns out that a piece isn't what it's supposed to be, you will have your money refunded.

However, the fact of the matter is, by the time a particular piece has worked its way through the trade, from the bottom to the top of the market, there's little or no (immediate) profit left in it. Consequently, to find more instantly profitable bargains from you will have to concentrate nearer the lower or less exclusive end of the market, such as market traders and small general antiques dealers. If you haven't already done so, you should read Chapter One (see pages 14-25) for a full description of the various types of antiques dealer, and an explanation of how they buy and sell to and from each other and the general public.

Making a quick or short-term profit on an antique or collectable bought from a market trader or a small general antique dealer is dependent on the following factors:

1. Spotting something that has been under priced: as in other fields of business, many antique dealers are not experts on everything they sell. A small general dealer might, for example, be very knowledgeable about ceramics and abreast of their current market price. On the other hand, he or she may not know that much about silver, or glass. You can capitalize on this if your knowledge is greater than theirs. For example, there is a lovely story going back a few years of a lady browsing in a small antique shop in Dorset. She came across a small, carved wooden stick, which was rather ugly, to say the least, embellished with a disproportionately large head and a grimacing face. She snapped it up for £4, much to the amusement of the rest of her family, and immediately took it up to Phillips in London, where it was confirmed as an extremely rare, mid-19th-century, Hawaiian god stick. She was understandably delighted when it fetched £15,700 at auction.

2. Being able to sell it on for more elsewhere: as described in Chapter One (see pages 14-25), 'runners' make most of their living by buying from a dealer in one area and selling for a higher price to a dealer in another area.

They, and you, can do this if you know that a particular piece is more valuable in one part of the country than another. For example, Tunbridgeware has always been more sought after in Tunbridge Wells, where it was originally made, than elsewhere. Consequently, if you can find it, you will pay less for it from a dealer in Yorkshire than you can sell it for in Kent. Runners also make their money by buying from dealers who have clients with shallow pockets and selling to dealers who have clients with deep pockets. In other words, the average clientele of a small antique shop in a provincial town or village will usually pay less for something than the people who patronize a shop in Bond Street. If you can buy in the village shop for £50, you may be able to sell to the Bond Street dealer for £100. (He, in turn, will of course put it in his window for a lot more.) Similarly, if you have contacts with collectors they may well be prepared to pay 'over the odds' if they really covet something very special.

3. Being able to 'improve' it: if you spot something on a market stall or in a dealer's shop that is in need of repair, you may be able to clean it or restore it and thus enhance its value. Restoring antiques can be both time-consuming and expensive. Consequently, many dealers prefer to sell something on quickly 'as is', rather than tie money up and incur additional costs improving it. If you feel you can restore something properly and economically, you may be able to make money on it. However, this is an area rife with both opportunities and dangers, and you should refer to Chapter Five (see pages 110-131) before proceeding.

4. Matching it up with something already owned: as a general rule, sets of something are worth disproportionately more than singles. Consequently, if you already have seven Chippendale chairs and you see a matching chair in an antique shop, by buying it and making a set of eight you will be able to sell the set for much more than the seven. Similarly, if you have 51 cigarette cards and you spot the 52nd that makes the complete set, it will invariably be worth buying. The incomplete set is worth less than half of the complete set. The same is true of ceramics; a pair of vases is always worth more than two singles. Whether you are buying for short-term profit or long-term investment, and regardless of the type of dealer you are buying from, you will obviously want to buy for the best possible price. In order to do this you:

1. Need to be able to speak the same language as the person you're dealing or 'haggling' with. Indeed, if you can pass yourself off as 'trade' you should be able to secure a better discount on the advertised price than a member of the public. Most dealers will knock off about 10 per cent, but some may offer more, particularly if their stock is priced for the tourist market. There is a glossary at the back of the book called 'Tradespeak' (see page 162). You should familiarise yourself with many of the turns-of-phrase included before negotiating in earnest. Bear in mind, while you should ask each and every dealer 'what's your best price?', barrow-boy language might work in a London market, but it won't go down well in Harrogate or the West End. You have to adapt your language to fit the situation.

2. Buy at the right time. At open markets and many antique fairs, much of the day's trading is done early in the morning, and most of it between dealers. Bermondsey market in London, for example, starts at 5am. As with boot fairs and jumble sales, get there early before all the bargains have been snapped up.

Finally, how do you protect yourself against buying fakes and forgeries? As already discussed, buying from a registered B.A.D.A. or L.A.P.A.D.A. dealer should be insurance enough. As far as other sources are concerned, my advice to you is rely on your own knowledge and expertise, rather than automatically accepting someone else's description or opinion. In theory, antiques, like most other commodities, come under the Trades Descriptions Act, and any dealer falsely describing something is legally liable to recompense you. However, in practice seeking legal redress can be an expensive business, particularly with something as ambiguous as the provenance of antiques. You should also know that while antiques sold through auction are invariably described in good faith, technically they do not come under the Trades Descriptions Act. However, the advent of V.A.T. on the buyer's premium means the auction house is providing a service, and thus liable to refund your money if you can prove they have incorrectly described a lot.

CHAPTER FIVE

CLEANING, REPAIR AND RESTORATION

———————— £ ————————

Almost without exception, any antique or collectable in good condition is more sought after, and therefore more valuable, than a similar example that is dirty and uncared for, or in need of repair or restoration. However, cleaning, repairing and restoring antiques is an area fraught with dangers, particularly for the over-enthusiastic amateur or someone new to the trade. During the years I have been involved with antiques I have come across numerous horror stories, and these tend to fall into two main categories:

First, there are instances of someone cleaning a piece – usually an item of furniture, such as a bureau or a chest of drawers – and restoring it to supposedly pristine condition, only to discover when they come to sell it that they have sub-stantially reduced, rather than increased, its value. The reason for this is nearly always the same: they've gone too far, and stripped away the patina of age – namely, the dust, dirt and pol-ish, the effects of exposure to light and shade, and the natural wear and tear that accumulates over the years to produce a subtle, lustrous finish on the surface of a piece. It is, of course, upon such a patination that much of the value of an antique depends. Decades, even centuries, of patination, particularly on items of furniture, can be all-too-easily wiped out at a stroke by injudicious use of cleaning agents in the hands of the unwary or the unskilled. Second, there are examples of some-one tackling quite complicated repairs – such as remodelling and hand-painting a missing arm etc. from a Meissen figure, reassembling a Chippendale chair, or repairing sections of marquetry on a Dutch table – and making a bodge of it by using the wrong materials and techniques and/or by, quite simply, not being good enough at it. Restoring something properly often requires specialist skills that in many cases take years to acquire. Moreover, a badly restored piece will fetch less than an 'honest' unrestored one.

It is partly because of these dangers that many antiques dealers, particularly those in the lower echelons of the trade, tend to stick to a general rule of thumb: namely, if you are thinking of selling on a piece, don't make any repairs or restorations to it before offering it for sale. Precedent says the potential customer, whether it be another dealer or a private collector, would rather assess the authenticity and desirability of a piece in an unrestored condition, together with how much it will cost them to have it properly restored, rather than have to determine where repairs have been made, how good they are and, if they are inadequately done, how much it will cost to put them right.

There is also the time and money involved in restoration to be taken into account. If you want to make money out of antiques, there's no point in spending days – time is money – working on a piece, only to increase its value by a small percentage. (This is one of the reasons why it is extremely important to attend auctions regularly and look around antique shops, in order to keep up-to-date on prices. Specifically, you need to know the price difference between similar restored and unrestored items.)

Re-upholstering furniture, which can be a costly business, provides the perfect example of the financial risks involved in spending time and money on a complete restoration: many antique dealers may re-upholster an armchair or a sofa before putting it on display, but only to the point of fitting the calico undercover. This is because if they were to add an expensive top cover at this stage a potential customer will almost invariably say it was either the 'wrong' colour, pattern or fabric, and the sale will thus be lost. It is far better to secure the sale on the basis of providing the fabric of the customer's choice for an additional sum (or, if they prefer, letting the customer provide it themselves).

Equally, unless you are dealing at the upper-middle or top end of the trade, and therefore have a clientele who can absorb a relatively high mark-up, the cost of high-quality professional restoration will make it difficult to sell a particular piece for a decent profit, at least in the short term. This is not to say, however, that high-quality, professional restoration isn't worth it – provided you are certain you can sell the finished article. For example, I know of one dealer who specialises in Victorian furniture and over the years has bought numerous 19th-century sewing tables at auction, of which many have been in need of substantial repair. He employs, on a freelance basis, a top quality restorer to repair them, and pays him, on average, as much again as he bought the tables for. However, because the dealer knows he can sell the restored tables for between 500 and 800% more than he originally paid, forking out for restoration is well worth his while.

So, the best advice for anyone thinking of buying an antique in need of restoration is:

1. Assess whether you can make a decent profit by simply selling it on 'as is', rather than spend time and money on repairs that will show a poor return on your investment.

2. Determine the cost of a proper, professional restoration, add this to the purchase price and, if this still allows you to make a handsome profit when selling, put the piece in the hands of a good restorer. If you are thinking of buying and selling antiques

full-time, it is therefore important to cultivate working relationships with professional restorers in the areas you specialise in. While there are some good general restorers around, high-quality work is best carried out by a specialist in a particular field – furniture, ceramics, metal wares etc. An organisation well worth contacting in this respect is The United Kingdom Institute For Conservation: The British Antiques Furniture Restorer's Association (B.A.F.R.A.). Other antique dealers will also be able to recommend restorers, although you might have to sweet talk them a bit as they can be somewhat proprietorial towards skilled craftsmen whom they have used for many years and who offer them a priority service.

3. Don't attempt any major restorations yourself, unless you have acquired the necessary skills. There are various specialist books on the market that aim to teach you how to restore all manner of antiques, and many of them tackle sophisticated projects, such as re-upholstering sofas and settees, re-caning chairs, repairing porcelain and clocks, and re-welding metal wares etc. By all means try your hand at such repairs and restorations. You may discover you have an aptitude for the work. However, don't practise on anything of real value, or it may well turn out to be an expensive learning process. Indeed, a very experienced furniture dealer I know advises anybody who asks him about whether they should tackle furniture repairs: 'don't even try, unless you're the sort of person who can saw a dead straight line in all planes' – if you've never tried this, have a go on some off-cuts of wood and you'll be surprised how difficult it is.

4. Do, however, consider cleaning up and making very minor repairs to a piece to improve its general appearance and therefore value and saleability. There are various things you can do to achieve this, without causing damage and without having to resort to professional help. Over the following pages is a description of various, traditional techniques used by dealers to increase the profitability of certain antiques. It is by no means a comprehensive list, and you should refer to the numerous specialist books on cleaning, repair and restoration if you wish to tackle more of these things yourself. However, none of the following 'tricks of the trade' are especially time-consuming or expensive, nor are they that risky – provided you always exercise caution and call in a professional if at all in doubt.

REMOVING MARKS OFF FURNITURE

Bleaching

To counteract bleaching brought about by excessive exposure to sunlight, apply teak oil with a cotton wool ball, gently rubbing it into the grain. Allow to dry for approximately a couple of days, then repeat the application until the original colour of the wood is restored. At this point, polish the surface with a traditional furniture polish (a hard polish for solid woods and a lighter, cream polish for more delicate veneers).

Bloom

To get rid of a bloom – a soft grey blush of colour– that appears on the surface of wax-polished, lacquered and varnished wooden surfaces (usually because the above finishes were applied on a slightly damp surface), gently apply either a light coat of a proprietary white wax polish or a small quantity of oil of spike.

Bruises and dents

To reduce bruises and dents on the surface of wood, begin by removing excess polish from the surface by gently wiping down with turpentine or white spirit. Then lay two or three folds of a damp cloth over the damaged area and place an iron (set at a low temperature) on top of them. Keep this in place for approximately 30 seconds, remove, examine the underlying surface, and repeat at intervals until the bruise or dent has virtually disappeared, all the time making sure the surface doesn't become too hot. Once you are satisfied, allow to dry thoroughly, then repolish. Do not attempt this on particularly valuable pieces of furniture – that is best left to professionals.

Candle wax

To remove candle wax, wrap crushed ice in muslin and place it over the affected area for a few minutes. (This will make the wax more brittle.) Remove the ice and carefully scrape off the wax with your fingernail or a wooden spatula. Once the surface has dried, lightly buff with polish and a soft cloth.

Fly marks

To remove the little black specks left on the surface by insects such as flies, brush them off with a hog's bristle brush, gently scratch them off with your fingernail, carefully lift them with the blade of a craft knife or, if they are particularly stubborn, cover them for approximately ten minutes with a piece of cotton wool soaked in linseed oil, and then brush them off.

Grime

To remove sticky dirt and grime that has accumulated on the surface of an uncared-for piece that has been uncared-for for years, either apply a proprietary furniture cleaner with cotton wool (and a soft brush for crevices), or mix up the following:

4 parts turpentine (or white spirit)
4 parts white vinegar
4 parts boiled linseed oil
1 part methylated spirits
3 or 4 drops of ammonia

and apply in the same way. This mixture will also help to revive the underlying polish.

Ink

Remove wet ink with a damp cloth. Dried ink presents more of a problem: using cotton wool buds, apply either a little white vinegar, lemon juice with salt, or a weak solution of oxalic acid (which is poisonous), and rinse with water immediately afterwards. If none of these work, you could cautiously try a weak solution of bleach, again applied with a cotton wool bud and rinsed thoroughly afterwards.

Once dry, the now slightly paler treated area can be re-coloured with boot polish or a little wood stain, and then repolished carefully..

Oil and grease

To remove cooking oils, butter and cream etc., wipe immediately with a soft cloth and then lightly repolish. Shift older stains with cotton wool soaked in a little white spirit, before repolishing the piece.

Metal fittings

Before cleaning any metal fittings in situ, mask off the surrounding areas with pieces of plastic sheeting or stiff card (held in place with masking tape). Light rust on iron or steel can be removed by gently rubbing with fine grade emery paper and a little light lubricating oil.

Heavy rust needs to be soaked for a while with a rust remover, then rinsed with white spirit. Once rust has been removed from iron or steel, the surface should be given a thin coat of either white wax polish or lanolin. Brass should be cleaned with a proprietary brass cleaner or by gently rubbing over with crocus powder.

Mother-of-pearl

Protect the surrounding areas before cleaning mother-of-pearl, bone, and coloured and semi-precious stones used for decorative inlay in furniture. To remove a build-up of wax, carefully apply, with a cotton wool bud, a little of the mixture used to remove grime on furniture (see above). Then, bleach away remaining stains either with a little hydrogen peroxide (strength: 20% volume) or, if they are stubborn, a paste of whiting and hydrogen peroxide (again: 20% volume). In both cases, gently rub the solution or paste across the inlay with a cotton wool bud. Finally, rinse with water, dry with a cloth and polish with white wax.

Ormolu

Tarnished ormolu is best removed from the piece of furniture before treating. However, if you have to leave it in place, carefully mask off the surrounding area before proceeding. Mix a solution of:

2 pints distilled water
1oz caustic soda
3oz sodium potassium tartrate.

Because of the caustic nature of this solution, you must wear rubber gloves and plastic goggles to protect hands and eyes. Apply the mixture with a nylon brush, leave for a couple of minutes, then rinse off with water. Finally, buff up with a chamois leather (don't use a metal polish, as it will damage the surface of the ormolu). Very mildly tarnished ormolu can sometimes be cleaned quite effectively by washing down with warm soapy water and a spoonful of white vinegar.

Paint

Remove wet or touch-dry oil paint with a rag and white spirit. Dry oil paint needs an application of paint stripper, which should be scraped off, together with the softened paint, after about half a minute. Then gently rub in a circular motion over the affected area with cotton wool moistened with white spirit. This will slightly dissolve the surrounding polish and help to fill the depression left by the stripper. Finally, apply a little teak oil or boot polish to revive the colour, before repolishing.

Treat hardened emulsion paint in the same way, although wet emulsion (and wet acrylics) can be removed with a damp cloth. Dry acrylic paint can be shifted with cotton wool moistened with methylated spirits and placed over the affected area for approximately half an hour. Once soft, carefully remove the paint with your fingernail or a wooden spatula, and then repair the surface as for oil paints (see above).

Parquetry

To remove layers of dulled polish from parquetry work, apply the cleaning mixture specified for removing grime (see above), working carefully on a small area at a time and removing the excess with cotton wool moistened with white spirit. Then, if necessary, carefully wipe over with a little methylated spirits, followed by more white spirit. Finally, apply a small amount of teak oil and, 24 hours later, repolish the surface.

Tar

Gently warm hardened tar, then remove as much as you can with dry cotton wool, before wiping off the rest with a cloth moistened with either turpentine or eucalyptus oil.

Water marks

You will need to be persistent and patient, but glass ring-marks can be removed by applying a mixture of:

4 parts linseed oil
1 part turpentine

having first simmered the linseed oil for approximately a quarter of an hour, allowed it to cool, and then added the turpentine. (Do this outside as there is a fire risk, plus the fumes given off by the simmering linseed can be fairly unpleasant.) Then, soak some cotton wool in the mixture and place over the affected area for about half a day. Finally, remove the pad of cotton wool, wipe off the area with a cloth and repolish. For very small spots of discolouration, a gentle application of white vinegar often works.

Scratches and abrasions

To disguise light scratches and abrasions apply a proprietary scratch remover. This will slightly dissolve the layers of wax polish which will, when they harden again, form a smoother and more attractive surface.

MAKING MINOR REPAIRS TO FURNITURE

Canework

To strengthen weakened areas of canework, liberally brush on a mixture of:

1 part acrylic matt medium
1 part water

Apply up to two or three coats, allowing the surface to dry before applying the next one. Next, dissolve a small quantity of purified, bleached beeswax in benzine and rub this into the cane with a cloth. Allow to dry for one hour, then buff with a soft cloth. Discoloured canework can be cleaned with a weak solution of soap and water prior to strengthening.)

Cracks

Fill small cracks by first cleaning out any debris with an old toothbrush. Next, heat a little beeswax until it is soft and pliable, knead in a matching dry powder colour and rub into the crevices with a cloth. Once hardened, buff up the affected and surrounding areas and repolish. Larger cracks need to be part-filled with a proprietary wood filler (of matching colour) before applying the coloured wax.

French polish

Minor scratches in a French-polished surface can be filled with tinted wax (as above). Where the polish has acquired an all-over, slightly abrasive 'mossy' appearance, it can be revived by applying sparingly with a cloth, and, using gentle pressure and a circular motion, the following mixture:

3 parts raw linseed oil
4 parts methylated spirits
2 parts turpentine (or white spirit)
1 part beeswax

Shake up the wax, methylated spirits and turpentine in a container until the wax has dissolved in the mixture, and then add the linseed.

Stopping small holes

To fill small holes either use a proprietary stopper tinted to the same colour as the wood, or mix a little sawdust with a synthetic adhesive to form a paste, which can then be tinted with a dry powder colour. Because these mixtures shrink when dry, fill the holes proud of the surrounding surface and, when the filler has dried, carefully sand down with fine-grade sandpaper. Finally, repolish the surface.

Woodworm

Treat woodworm and other insect infestation with a propri-etary solution (usually in liquid from), always working in a well-ventilated area and protecting hands and eyes with gloves and goggles. Once treated, further infestation can be thwarted by a regular application of a proprietary polish containing an anti-woodworm (beetle) ingredient.

REVIVING AND POLISHING FURNITURE

In addition to removing encrusted dirt and grime from furniture (see above), you may have acquired some pieces that would benefit from a simple clean and polish. You can do this quite easily by:

1. Washing down the piece with a piece of towelling that has been dipped in warm, soapy water and then thoroughly wrung out until almost dry. Keep changing the soap and water as it becomes dirty.

2. Rinsing any soap residue with another towel that has been dipped in clean warm water and, as before, thoroughly wrung out. Again, keep changing the water as it becomes dirty.

3. Drying the surface thoroughly with clean, dry towelling.

4. Polish the surface with a soft cloth, lightly impregnated with a furniture polish containing beeswax. Apply the polish sparsely and evenly over the whole surface. Allow to dry for a minimum of twenty minutes, then buff with a clean soft cloth, working in a circular motion and applying an even pressure across the entire surface.

CLEANING CERAMICS

Removing stains

Providing the underlying glaze is sound you can remove tea and coffee stains from china by soaking them in a solution of:

2oz borax
1 pint water

gently rubbing away the stains with a bottle brush, and then rinsing thoroughly with water. (However, fine-quality porcelain should be left to a professional as there is a substantial risk of damaging the glaze.)

Grey-brown stains left by mildew and mould can be shifted with a weak solution of bleach.

Washing

Before washing china, carefully check for any damage to the glaze or previous repairs, and don't proceed if you find any. If everything is sound, fill a large plastic bowl with warm water – no hotter than the temperature of a baby's bath – and add a little liquid soap.

Carefully lower one piece into the water and very gently rub it all over with a soft cloth, using a soft, long-haired brush in any recesses. Remove the piece and very gently slush it around in a second bowl of warm water (same temperature as before), before gently drying it with a soft cloth.

If there are any marks that prove stubborn during the first stage, these can often be shifted by rubbing a little neat soap directly into them.

CLEANING METALS

Brass

Remove marks by mixing a little paraffin with jeweler's rouge to form a liquid paste, and then gently rubbing it over the affected area with a soft cloth. (It is advisable to wear gloves and goggles to protect hands and eyes from the inflammatory effects of the rouge.)

Remove severe corrosion with a fairly strong solution of washing soda, again wearing gloves and goggles for protection. To protect brass from further corrosion, apply either a thin coat of fine white wax polish or a proprietary lacquer.

Bronze

Exercising extreme caution (so as not to destroy the patina), first dust down the object with a soft brush. Then remove grease and dirt from any recesses and details, using a brush dipped in a little white spirit. Once clean, polish as for brass (see above). Leave removing verdigris to a professional.

Chrome

Remove rust stains with a soft cloth and a proprietary cleaner and chrome polish, but don't rub too hard or you may cut through to the underlying metal. To remove dirt, gently wash with a little soapy water (adding a drop of ammonia if there is any discoloration present). Then, rinse in clean water and dry.

Copper

To remove verdigris mix a solution of:
1/2oz citric acid
1 pint warm water
and wash it over the affected area with a sponge. Then, rinse with warm soapy water, followed by just warm water, before drying thoroughly with a towel.

Iron

Remove surface rust with a little paraffin, rinse with white spirit, dry thoroughly and then protect against further rust by applying a white wax polish.

Lead

Restrict yourself to brushing down with a stiff-bristled brush.

Pewter

Restrict yourself either to rubbing it down gently with a soft chamois leather, or gently wiping it with a soft rag that has been slightly impregnated with a light clear oil and a little cro-cus powder. Then wipe down with cotton wool dipped in methylated spirits. Finally, wash down with warm soapy water, rinse thoroughly and dry with a soft cloth or piece of towelling.

Sheffield plate

Clean and polish using liquids and pastes, but never rub too hard or you may well 'cut' through the thin layer of silver. Wear thin cotton gloves when polishing.

Silver

Normal cleaning and polishing should be carried out with a proprietary silver polish (again, wearing thin cotton gloves). To remove tea and coffee stains, mix a solution of:

1 tsp. borax
1 pint hot water

Pour this into the receptacle and leave for a couple of hours. Then, gently rub over the affected areas with a soft brush, empty the borax solution, wash out with warm soapy water, rinse with clean water and, finally, dry with a piece of cloth.

CLEANING GLASS

Chandeliers

Assuming they are not connected up to the electricity, clean the glass with either a solution of hot water, a little methylated spirits and white vinegar, or hot water, a little detergent and a couple of drops of ammonia. (Wear gloves and goggles to pro-tect your hands and eyes.) Then, dry thoroughly.

Enamelled glass

Begin by gently cleaning with a soft chamois leather slightly moistened with methylated spirits. Then very gently dry.

Engraved glass

Remove dirt and dust from recesses either with a soft brush or a soft brush dipped in a little methylated spirits.

Liquid containers

To remove the residue left by alcohol and other liquids pour in white vinegar and approximately 2tsp salt. Shake up the solution, leave for a couple of hours, pour out, rinse with clean water, and dry thoroughly (a hair-dryer, on a low setting, is very helpful for drying narrow-necked vessels).

Mirrors

Clean either with a soft cloth moistened with a little methylated spirits or a soft cloth and a little paraffin.

Stained glass

Clean off dirt and grime by gently washing down with warm water and a few drops of ammonia. Use either a soft cloth or, for heavy grime, a soft scrubbing brush. Then rinse with clean water, before drying thoroughly.

CLEANING JEWELRY

Amber

Gently wash in warm, soapy water. Thoroughly rinsed and dried, wipe on a little olive oil with cotton wool, then wipe off.

Aquamarine

Gently wash with tepid, soapy water, rinse and dry.

Cameos

Remove grease with a small artist's brush dipped in white spirit. Next brush over the affected area with a solution of warm soapy water plus a couple of drops of ammonia. Then, rinse by brushing on clean water, before drying with a piece of chamois leather.

Coral
Remove grime with cotton buds dipped in a solution of warm water plus a little detergent. Remove stubborn deposits with a paste of crocus powder and water, again gently applied with a cotton wool bud. Finally, rinse with clean water and dry.

Diamanté
Clean by lightly wiping with a soft brush dipped in alcohol. Dry immediately by blowing over the surface.

Diamonds
Wash in warm soapy water, removing stubborn grease and grime by brushing on a little methylated spirits and ammonia.

Emeralds
Gently wash in a solution of warm soapy water and a couple of drops of ammonia. Stubborn grime can be shifted by gently brushing on a little methylated spirits, prior to rinsing and drying with a soft cloth.

Ivory
Limit yourself to wiping down with a soft cloth moistened with warm water and a little detergent. Then wipe down with clean water and dry thoroughly. Finally, if desired, wipe on a little almond oil, leave for a couple of minutes, and then wipe off.

Jade
Clean with a soft cloth moistened with warm, soapy water and a couple of drops of ammonia. to get into any crevices.

Jet

Clean by gently rubbing with pieces of fresh bread. This, unusual, method really works wonders at bringing out the shine of a piece of jet.

Opals

Clean with cotton buds dipped in warm, soapy water. Rinse by applying clean water with cotton buds, then dry.

Pearls

Clean artificial pearls with a damp chamois leather. Clean real pearls by placing them in a jar containing potato flour, gently shaking the jar for a couple of minutes, leaving for about a day, shaking again, leaving for another day, giving them a final shake, removing them from the jar and brushing off the powder with a soft brush.

Rubies

Clean by gently rubbing with a cotton wool bud dipped in warm soapy water. Then rinse and dry thoroughly, before lightly wiping down with a piece of chamois leather moistened with alcohol.

Sapphires

Clean in the same way as for rubies (above).

Tortoiseshell

Wash with warm soapy water, rinse and dry thoroughly. Then, either apply a fine, white wax polish, or wipe on a little almond oil.

Turquoise

Clean with a cotton wool bud dipped in methylated spirits.

CLEANING TEXTILES

I would advise anyone contemplating cleaning antique textiles to pay a professional to carry out the work, as it is all too easy to cause irreversible damage and thus substantially detract from their value.

However, it is possible to remove various stains, provided you always: test the surface for colour-fastness by carefully applying the specified cleaning agent (or bleach) to a small patch at the edge of the item in question – if any colour runs, employ a professional to sort out the problem; use distilled rather than tap water, whenever water is specified; and work in a circle – out to in – so as to avoid leaving a ring mark.

Alcohol (spirits)

Remove with clean water if still damp. If dry, rub in a solution of warm water and mild detergent with your fingertips. Then rinse and allow to dry naturally.

Beer

If the textile is white-coloured, you can use a weak bleach, consisting of:
1 part 20% volume hydrogen peroxide
6 parts water
then rinse and allow to dry.

Beetroot

Gently apply a solution consisting of:
1oz borax
1 pint warm water.

Blood

Employ a professional.

Candle wax

Surround the area with brown wrapping paper, and apply a fairly hot iron. Keep replacing the paper and reapplying the iron until the worst has gone. Then remove the remaining traces with a little white spirit.

Chocolate

Remove the worst with a plastic spatula, then treat as for beetroot (as above).

Coffee

If still damp, remove as for beetroot (see above). Remove dry stains by rubbing gently with glycerine, leaving for approximately one hour, rinsing with water and then washing with warm, soapy water.

Fats and oil

Light stains can be removed by dabbing with a little white spirit. Heavy stains should be treated in the same way as candle wax (see above).

Fruit juice

Remove by dabbing with a little lemon juice and then washing with water. Treat as for beetroot if the stain is stubborn.

Ink

Remove ball-point with either methylated spirits or, if that doesn't work, petroleum. Remove felt-tip with a little methylated spirits, and then wash with warm soapy water.,

Iron mould

To remove, place a rag under the marks (if at all possible), then dab on a 2% solution of Chloramine T, leave for approximately one minute, then rinse with distilled water. Next, dab on a 2% solution of oxalic acid (poisonous) and distilled water, leave for approximately one minute, then rinse thoroughly with distilled water. Dry the surface as much as possible by dabbing with white blotting paper, before allowing to dry naturally. (There are also various proprietary rust stain removers on the market and you might like to try them as an alternative, rather than have your chemist mix up the above solutions.)

Mildew
Clean with a proprietary cleaner.

Milk
Wash with warm soapy water and, if necessary, repeat having added a little borax to the water. (You can also use a mild bleach on white materials.)

Nail varnish
Remove with methylated spirits or, use acetone.

Paints
Remove damp acrylics with water. If dry, place a pad of cotton wool moistened with methylated spirits on top of the affected area. Leave for approximately ten minutes, then wash away with water.

Remove emulsions with methylated spirits. Remove oils with white spirit if still wet. If dry, gently dab on a little paint stripper (wearing gloves and goggles to protect hands and eyes) with a cotton wool bud. Immediately the paint starts to wrinkle dab on some white spirit and remove the paint with a small brush (such as an old toothbrush). Then rinse with warm soapy water, followed by warm clean water, and allow to dry.

Scorch marks

Wash the affected area with a warm solution of:

2oz borax
1 pint water

followed by a weak solution of bleach. As an alternative you might also like to try rubbing the area with a freshly cut onion and then soaking it in cold water.

Shoe polish

Gently rub the affected area with a swab of cotton wool which has been moistened with a little white spirit.

CHAPTER SIX

HOW TO SELL

—————————— £ ——————————

I've already discussed, in previous chapters, how making money out of antiques is heavily dependent on knowing where and what to buy, but, to maximise your profit, you also need to know where and how to sell. As with buying, there are a number of outlets open to you, and the one you choose will depend on various factors: namely, whether you are dealing full- or part-time, how competitive a price you bought the piece(s) for in the first place, whether you need to realise a quick profit or can afford to wait until the market is 'just right', and, as with most things in life, who you know or get to know (i.e. your network of contacts in the trade, with collectors and among the general public).

Before looking at the different outlets for selling antiques and collectables, it is important to consider various aspects of selling in general. In many respects there are few differences between selling antiques and any other commodity: you try to buy for a competitive price, keep your overheads under control and sell for a reasonable profit, while all the time trying to both retain and expand your clientele. Success on the selling and expansion side invariably comes down to providing a good service. This involves presenting your products in a favourable a light (while remaining honest about them), developing a rapport with your clients and selling for the right price.

What is the right price? Well, you could say 'as much as anybody is prepared to pay', but that isn't particularly helpful when it comes to putting on a price tag (although 'how much two or more people are prepared to pay' does hold good for auctions). As a generalisation, most professional dealers try to make between 30% and 60% across the board (their mark-up on the purchase price being both overheads and profit). However, on lower-priced items, around 100% can be nearer the mark, while on higher-priced pieces as low as 20% and 25% is not unusual. Of course, profits on particular pieces can be way in excess of such figures if you have been lucky or clever enough to have bought something for a bargain price in the first place, or if they have become more collectable and valuable during the intervening period.

With all these variables, therefore, the only sure-fire way of pricing something correctly is to keep abreast of the current market values (both at auction, in shops and on stalls) – bearing in mind that, as on the stock exchange, you will rarely beat the market. Moreover, in my experience, precedent says you shouldn't be too greedy. By keeping your prices competitive (which you need to do anyway, to survive), you are more likely to achieve a fast and high turnover. In the long run this can be more profitable than holding out for higher prices. For example, it is better to sell two £40 pieces every week throughout the year at a 20% mark up, than two £200 items a year with a 60% mark up. If you take the first approach you will make £832; if you take the second you will make only £480. (Of course, this has to be qualified: it only works if you can keep replenishing your stock at the required rate.)

As for presenting your products in as favourable a light as possible, this almost goes without saying. However, you only have to go to an antiques fair or into a few dealers shops to discover instantly that some people are much better at displaying their wares than others.

It is perhaps no coincidence that, from a buyer's point of view, most bargains are found on poorly laid out stalls or in shambolic shops, whereas, from a seller's viewpoint, the best prices are obtained from attractively presented stalls, appealing and enticing shop displays.

If you're selling, you will need to master the art of display. In many respects it is akin to flower-arranging: some people have a natural aptitude for it, and others don't. If you are one of the former, you're off to a flying start. If you're in the latter category you should take heart from the fact that, with a little thought and commitment, you will be able to acquire the necessary skills. Studying other people's displays is the quickest way to learn the art of effectively positioning pieces in relation to one another, and, later in the chapter, I mention specific ideas that have stood antique dealers in good stead in the past.

So far as developing a rapport with customers is concerned, I would even go as far as to say that this is the most important factor in successful selling, especially in a business where so much of the trading is done face-to-face.

The plain fact of the matter is, most people prefer dealing with people they like. Consequently, they are more likely to buy pieces from you if you are helpful, polite, friendly and enthusiastic, than if you are off-hand and just let the pieces speak for themselves.

That's not to say the latter approach won't work with some items if customers – such as an avid collector – are desperate to buy them. This occasion is usually rare, however, and it is far more important to learn how to deal successfully with a wider range of potential buyers.

In fact, it would be true to say that there is an art to successful selling and, as an old dealer friend once said to me, 'there's a world of difference between selling and helping 'someone to buy'. In other words, you can either talk someone into buying something you have for sale – what could be described as a 'hard sell' – or you can find out what they want or need and then try to match it to your stock.

Auctions

Selling pieces at auction does not, of course, require any selling technique so far as the potential buyer is concerned. The piece(s) will either sell or not sell, and how much it goes for will depend on who is bidding and how much he, she or they are prepared to go up to – although when it comes to the sale the auctioneer will be trying to get as high a price as possible as he is selling on your behalf, and the more he gets for it, the more commission the auction house makes.

When you take in items to an auction house you will be asked if you wish to place a reserve on them; that is, a minimum price below which you are not prepared to sell. I recommend you take up this option with all but the poorest of pieces, otherwise you could be unlucky – there might be only one person attending the sale who is interested in your lot(s) – and the bidding will never get off the ground. Putting on a reserve is also a way of protecting yourself against any 'ring' that might be in operation (see pages 104-5). The auction house will be able to advise you on an appropriate reserve for the piece(s) in question, although at the end of the day the minimum price set is up to you.

There are a number of costs involved in selling at auction. First, you will have to pay a seller's commission. This will vary between 10% and 15% of the hammer price, and is also subject to V.A.T.. Second, you pay for transport (also subject to V.A.T.) if you ask the auction house to pick up any pieces from your home or place of business (and return them if they remain unsold). The cost of carriage can vary considerably, depending on which part of the country you live in (London is the most expensive), and the number, size and weight of the pieces involved (a large wardrobe will obviously be more expensive than an occasional chair, for example). To give you an idea of the cost, a friend of mine recently sold an early 19th-century,

French provincial armoire at Phillips, in central London, and their delivery company charged £31.25 plus V.A.T. for picking it up from north London. Third, you will pay a small amount, plus V.A.T., for insurance (rarely more than £5 for anything up to £1,000). And fourth, the leading London auction houses usually charge a fee if a photograph of a particular piece is taken and used to illustrate the auction catalogue (this can be as much as £35 plus Value Added Tax).

So, it can be quite an expensive business selling items at auction, and you must take into account all of these costs when working out how much something needs to sell for to make it worth your while. However, the fact that so many dealers regularly sell through auctions means it is perfectly possible to make good money in this way, provided you bought at the right price in the first place. It is also a good means of turning over stock and keeping a fairly fluid cash-flow. Moreover, some auction houses charge a lower seller's commission to professional dealers than they do to members of the general public – although it is unlikely this will be volunteered, so you have to ask. Also, if an item fails to reach its reserve (and doesn't sell), most auction houses will either charge you a reduced commission – approximately $2\frac{1}{2}$% of the reserve price – or offer to put it into the next sale with a reduced reserve (or with none at all), and waive any commission from the original auction.

Finally, there are three old adages that most professional dealers take into account when selling through auction. The first is, avoid putting anything in a sale just after you have hawked it around the trade. If other dealers see something come up that they and their fellow professionals have recently declined to buy when approached on the phone or at their shop, they will assume you are pretty desperate to sell and therefore are unlikely to bid high. Second, the trade like nothing more than a 'fresh' piece; in other words, something that hasn't been seen before, or done the rounds, and therefore may still have a fair amount of profit in it (see Chapter One, pages 14-25, for an explanation of how individual pieces move from dealer to dealer). And third, if you are concerned about cash-flow, selling through suburban or country auction houses will ensure a quicker sale than going through the leading London salerooms. In the case of the latter, having taken your piece(s) in, you may have to wait three or four months before the next appropriate sale (and then a further month for the cheque to arrive). The former hold more regular sales (and often settle accounts quicker).

Friends

In Chapter Four (see pages 88-109) I have already talked about the pros and cons of buying antiques from friends and relatives. The chief lesson learned was, I hope: friendship is more important than profit. Much the same applies to selling, or selling on their behalf. With the former, anything that smacks of a 'hard sell' is inappropriate. If they want or need something you have in stock, or can get for them, that's fine. And, as you would with any other dealers (see below), offer a discount (between 10% and 20%, depending on your mark-up).

If they ask you to sell on their behalf this is worth considering, especially if you are short of capital. However, you should always stick to some fairly stringent ground rules:

1. Work on a sale-or-return basis.

2. Write everything down that you take away to sell, and include a description of each item with either an agreed minimum price and/or your percentage commission. Date the paper, and get them to sign it so that there can be no misunderstandings later on.

3. If you are working on commission, this should not be less than 25% if you want to make a reasonable profit.

4. Again, to avoid any misunderstandings, either put the pieces into auction or sell them to dealers from another area: you would be surprised at the resentment that can arise if your friend or relatives subsequently see 'their' possessions for sale in a local antique shop at a price well above what you gave for them – even if you have scrupulously stuck to 1-3 above, and tried to explain how the dealer you sold the pieces to has to add on his own mark-up if he is to make a living.

Car Boot Sales and Junk Shops

Car boot sales and junk shops are great places to look for bargains when buying antiques and collectables (as described in Chapters One and Four, see pages 14-25 and 88-109). However, unless you wish to dispose of various bits and pieces that you can't sell in any other way (probably because they aren't good enough), these are not generally suitable outlets for making a decent profit.

Although there are the occasional exceptions that prove the rule, most of the people who know about antiques are there looking for pieces that the seller's don't realise are valuable, and if they find them, will sell them on elsewhere – i.e., at auction, to dealers, or to members of the public at antiques fairs or through antiques shops.

From Home

Selling antiques from home can be an attractive proposition for the full- and part-time dealer alike. In Chapter One (see pages 14-25), I described how an increasing number of dealers have dispensed with an antique shop and all the attendant overheads – leases, staff, insurance, fuel bills, etc. – and started working from home. The advances in technology, notably the fax, mobile phone and laser copier (the latter allowing you to make very high-quality, colour images from photographic prints of your stock, which can then be posted or even faxed to your clients) have helped enormously in this area. As in many other lines of business, you're not cut-off in the way you tended to be in the past.

However, with no shop window to display your wares you will still have to get out and about to make yourself known. In Chapter Seven: Setting up in Business (see pages 150-161), I have described the importance of advertising, through local papers and trade magazines, together with distributing well-designed business cards, the aim to make yourself known and build up a regular customer base. Many successful dealers I know who work from home began like this. However, they also contacted specialist societies and antiques collectors' clubs. (*Antique Collecting: The Journal of the Antique Collector's Club* includes a list of regional antiques societies and clubs. Names and addresses are also often listed in trade periodicals and specialist magazines.) And they regularly took (and continue to take) stalls and stands at antiques fairs (see below) to not only sell their stock, but also to make themselves known to the rest of the trade and the public alike – in other words, at the outset, they put themselves about a bit.

Invariably, the dealers who have prospered have tended to specialise in one, or maybe two, specific areas, and their clients mainly consist of serious collectors who will be interested in most of the stock they carry. It does take time and effort to build up the sort of reputation that results in collectors ringing you more often than you ring them, but it can be lucrative.

One dealer informed me that over the years he has built up a rapport with most of his clients, and he is convinced that each of them feels they are his most important client. If this sounds cynical, it isn't. This chap really does provide a superb service – and that's one of the keys to succeeding in business. Depending on distance, he is often prepared to take pieces to clients' homes if they can't come to his. In addition, he runs what amounts to a mail-order service: issuing regularly up-dated, illustrated stock sheets and sending out pieces on a sale-or-return basis to well-established clients (a fair number of whom live overseas). However, with new clients he does pro-tect himself by making sure cheques have cleared before goods are despatched, and he makes refunds only if the goods are returned undamaged.

Even if you intend to deal only part-time from home (virtu-ally as a hobby), you should read Chapter Seven on Setting up in Business, because it does detail some of the problems you should beware of: notably, local planning restrictions and potential capital gains liabilities if and when you come to sell the house. However, as you will see, provided you are sensible, such problems can be avoided.

Local Fairs

Antiques fairs fall into a number of categories, and the type of fair you should consider attending as a stall holder will depend on whether you buy and sell antiques part-time, you are new to the trade or whether you are in the business of establishing yourself as a full-time professional antiques dealer. For anyone in all but the latter category, taking a stall at a local antiques fair – the sort held in a village or town hall, or a function room at a hotel, and run either by a commercial company or a local char-ity – is a good way to start, can be surprisingly lucrative, if you know what you're doing, and offers an ideal way to start to know others in the trade.

Forthcoming fairs are usually advertised in local newspa-pers, on local radio, in specialist antiques magazines (such as *The Antiques Trade Gazette*) and on fly posters. Hiring a stall for a day is not particularly expensive – the usual range is between £15 and £30, depending primarily on location. For more popular and regularly held events you may well have to join a waiting list. Usually, there are few restrictions on the items you can sell (unlike some of the larger provincial and national trade fairs – see below). However, the organisers of these events may well have a surfeit of traders dealing in a particular type of antique, and will give preference to someone who has something more unusual to offer.

Whatever you deal in, you will discover that competition for buyers is pretty fierce, even if it seems fairly civilised on the surface (most antique dealers tend to be pretty friendly). Consequently, as I said above, you must display your wares in as attractive and enticing a way as possible. To maximise your chances of selling, you should:

1. Make sure your stall is well lit. Take desk-lamps (preferably antique) plus an extension lead to augment overhead lighting and, in case a power socket isn't available, always pack a good supply of candles.

2. Take a plain white or dark-coloured cloth to cover the table provided. Patterned fabrics and bright colours tend to distract potential buyers when looking at your stock.

3. Pack everything carefully in newspapers and sturdy cardboard boxes when travelling to and from the fair, otherwise you could have several breakages on your hands.

4. Label or tag all items with as full and accurate a description (as much as space will allow), together with a price. (I'm always extremely irritated by unpriced pieces, and rarely bother to ask. I, in common with all potential customers, like to know where I stand when it comes to assessing whether something is worth the price and whether I can afford it.)

5. Take plenty of change with you, and keep it to hand throughout the day in either a cash-box or a zipped purse strapped around your waist. With smaller, less expensive items, most people pay in cash. Not having the right change is irritating for the customer and inconvenient for you if you have to approach other stall-holders to see if they can help you out.

6. If at all possible, take a friend along who can relieve you while you relieve yourself, have a bite to eat and take a look around the other stalls to check out what other people are selling and how much they are selling it for.

7. Keep a detailed record of everything you sell and how much it sold for. By doing this you will be able to assess, at the end of the day, what sells and what doesn't sell.

8. Whenever you make a sale, wrap the item (unless it is a piece of furniture) in, at the very least, tissue paper, and preferably an attractive, wrapping paper – good presentation doesn't stop after you've laid out your stall.

9. Always set up your stall as early as possible – preferably at least an hour before the fair opens. That hour can often be your most lucrative as trade buyers (who are usually let in before members of the public) and regular stall-holders will always check out your stock (particularly if you're a newcomer) and probably offer to buy various items (to supplement their own stock). You have to be very careful here: keen-eyed dealers will snap up anything they feel is underpriced, and they may offer you multiple deals that are not quite what they seem.

For example, someone might offer to buy that blue and white vase for your asking price (which they tell you is rather high), but only if you throw in the cup and saucer for half-price. If you want to make money out of antiques you've got to know what they know: the vase is priced about right (or maybe a little high), but the cup and saucer is quite collectable and, if anything, a bargain in the first place. My advice in this sort of situation is, unless you receive what you know is a reasonable or good offer (allowing for a 10%-20% discount to a fellow dealer), hold out: many unwary newcomers have often got carried away, taken what appears to be loads of money in no time at all, only to discover they've made far less profit than they had originally hoped for, and had to sit behind a depleted and unenticing display for the rest of the day.

10. Never take cheques from a buyer without an accompanying cheque card, or a cheque of an amount that exceeds the cheque card's guarantee.

11. Be vigilant. Thieves come in a variety of guises, and most of them don't look like thieves at all. Learning to deal with one or more customers while keeping a sharp eye on your stock is something of an art, although it's surprising how observant one can be when it comes to ones own property and livelihood.

12. Keep on good terms with the organiser of the fair. As a newcomer you are extremely unlikely to be given a stall in a prime position. However, as vacancies occur you may be offered something better ahead of someone else if the organiser likes you and doesn't particularly take to them.

Sticking to all of the above is important. Nevertheless, as with most things in life, there is a learning curve: you will soon discover that if you sell all your stock too quickly, it is probably underpriced, and if you sell barely anything at all its is almost certainly overpriced.

Provincial Fairs

Large provincial antique fairs, lasting for about a week and held in public halls or hotels, are more prestigious events than the local fairs or markets described above.

The standards expected of stall-holders are correspondingly higher, with vetting committees scrutinising displays for authenticity and date before the fair is opened to members of the public. The dateline for antiques is often rigorously applied, and is usually ascertained using the following criteria:

1. Furniture: pre-1830

2. Porcelain, silverware and glass: pre-1860

3. Carpets and jewelry: pre-1890
4. Pictures: pre-1900

All items must be properly tagged (with an accurate description and, usually these days, a price rather than a price code).

These fairs are not for the beginner, and stalls and stands can often be very expensive – sometimes they are well over £1,000. However, they are nearly always worth the initial outlay as they are attended in large numbers, and many potential customers – usually including serious collectors – have fairly deep pockets. However, the basic principles of pricing, display and selling are just about the same as for local fairs . If you start dealing in antiques full-time, you will be undoubtedly have to consider taking a stall or stand fairly regularly – and that can mean anywhere between two and 20 times a year (closer to the latter if you don't have a shop). Forthcoming events are advertised in specialist magazines and trade periodicals.

National and International Fairs

Held over a period lasting from a week to a fortnight, and located in prestigious venues such as Olympia in London, the National Exhibition Centre in Birmingham or top city hotels, these attract top dealers from around the world and are attended by many serious collectors and connoisseurs. The vetting of stalls and stands, which can cost more than £5,000 for a fortnight, is even more rigorous than at top provincial fairs. The quality of antiques on display is very high, and prices reflect this accordingly. Over a fortnight, tens-of-thousands, even millions, of pounds will have changed hands.

If you want to make it to the top echelons of the antiques trade, and stay there, you will eventually need to participate. The overheads are high, but so are the potential profits. Yet, again, the basic principles of selling are the same as at lesser events: put on an attractive display at the right price(s), be knowledgeable, helpful and enthusiastic towards potential customers, and network with other dealers to expand your contacts and customer base.

Shops

You know the way some people say they'd like to pack everything in and run a nice little pub in the country: no stress any more and the wonderful opportunity to mix business with pleasure. Well, it doesn't often work out like that. The reality is long hours, difficulty in getting away for a holiday, staff problems and ever-increasing overheads. Well, selling antiques through an antiques shop can be like that. If you are dealing in antiques part-time and want to expand into something more permanent, think long and hard before taking on a shop: it's time-consuming and, if you're fortunate to get hold of a lease in a prime location, expensive.

However, this is not to say that many people don't make a great success of them, and they do offer advantages that other outlets can't provide. For example, unlike dealing from home they allow you to present a permanent display of stock and, once you are established, provide a base where your customers (both buying and selling) can always find you.

Ultimately, whether or not you take on a shop should depend on two main considerations:

1. How much money you have to borrow to purchase a lease. In other words, you have to be confident that you can generate sufficient turnover and profit to meet your interest payments, while still being able to invest continually in new stock. If you can finance the initial purchase from your own capital that will make taking on a shop a more attractive proposition. However, I don't believe there's any point in risking your money if you can't secure the second requirement, which is namely a shop in a good location.

2. As with the domestic housing market, location can be everything. If you're tucked away in a back street of a small village or town, and are well off the tourist trail, you are unlikely to prosper – however cheap the lease. On the other hand, a prime location in a major city or town should attract a steady stream of regular customers and casual passers-by (the latter hopefully turning into regular customers).

So far as running a shop on proper business lines is concerned, you should turn to Chapter Seven: Setting up a Business (see pages 150-161). And, in terms of laying out your shop and displaying your stock in the best possible light, I recommend that you apply much the same principles as you would on a stall in an antique market or trade fair (as above). The object is to make it appear you have a high turnover of stock (and are therefore competitive in terms of price and being able to find new and desirable pieces). But above all, try to develop a welcoming atmosphere that makes the public (and other dealers) want to come back for more.

Antiques Markets

Primarily because of the relatively high overheads associated with shops, in recent years there has been a growth in the number of permanent antiques markets in towns and cities. Often, but not always, purpose-built, they allow antique dealers to trade under a communal roof while keeping their own, distinct identity by buying and selling from their own booths. In that sense, they are a cross between a stall and a shop.

Most of these markets tend to be very cohesive in terms of the quality (and price) of the goods sold. For example, Grays, in London, is very up-market, with all the booth-holders specialising in a wide variety of good-quality antiques and desirable collectables. Prices range, accordingly, from many tens to many thousands of pounds. On the other hand, some of the markets in provincial towns and city suburbs are made up of dealers buying and selling further down the quality and price scale.

Anyone new to the trade must be realistic: the booths in the top markets are highly sought after. Moreover, the committees – usually made up of the owners and representatives from the booth-holders – that approve or black-ball applications will expect you to come with a good reputation and the ability to offer high-quality stock. Even if you fulfil these criteria there will probably still be a long waiting list.

However, because the antiques for sale are generally less valuable than those found in somewhere like Grays, these markets are a better prospect for someone who hasn't been in the business for long. (When vacancies occur they are usually advertised in the local and trade press.)

The Back of a Car or a Van

Chapter One: The Antiques Trade (see pages 14-25) describes the important role that 'runners' play in the antiques trade, buying in one part of the country and selling in another. Many people make a nice living operating in this way, the keys to success being:

1. High and fast turn-over.
2. Never travelling with an empty (estate) car – there's no point in going up to Norfolk from London to buy stock with nothing in the back. You might as well fill it with stuff you can sell there, before stocking up for the return journey.
3. Concentrating on 'insider dealing' (again, see Chapter One) – buying from and selling to other dealers, and swapping stock so that no one has anything going stale on them.
4. Never begrudging the next dealer in the chain his profit.

In my experience, runners are a special breed. So far as selling is concerned, they have a 'barrow-boy' mentality (and I don't mean that perjoratively): keep moving, keep networking and keep making deals is the name of the game. If you fit the bill and can speak the language, give it a go. However, I would say that runners are born, not made. They also thrive on what amounts to a nomadic lifestyle – when it comes down to it, most people don't, preferring the comforts of home.

Prices and Profit

However good you are at the art of selling, it is important to remember that the amount of profit you can make on any particular piece will be determined by where you are selling from and who you are selling to. In other words, the piece you picked up for £200 at a provincial auction might well go for several thousand pounds in a Bond Street showroom, but it will pass hands for considerably less than that further down the dealer chain (see Chapter One for a full explanation of this). The plain fact of the matter is: some dealers trade from better locations and have a more affluent clientele than others – customers who not only have deep pockets, but will also pay for the privilege of buying from them rather than from somebody else. This has to do with (good) location, reputation and trust and, in some cases I suspect, plain snobbery.

I was told a story a few years ago that illustrates perfectly the importance of all four of these when it comes to making money out of antiques. I was with a dealer friend in Stow-on-the-Wold and admiring a particularly fine table in his shop. He said it was the second time he'd had it for sale. A few years earlier he'd bought it at auction very cheaply and decided that he could offer it for sale at a reasonable price while still making a decent mark-up. Within a few days a couple came in from Broadway and showed considerable interest in his recent purchase. He offered to deliver it to their house so they could look at it in situ (an approach that normally results in a successful sale). However, after talking among themselves they declined the offer and said they would get back to him, but they never did. A week later a runner came in and bought the table for the asking price.

Another year passed, when the lady who had been interested in the table came into the shop. She said her husband had died and she wanted to sell various pieces. The dealer went to her house and, to his surprise, noticed 'his' table. The lady then showed him a receipt for it from a very eminent dealer in Broadway. This revealed the couple had paid over twice as much for the privilege of buying the table from a smart, well-established shop.

CHAPTER SEVEN

SETTING UP IN BUSINESS

——————— £ ———————

So, you have become quite knowledgeable about antiques. The old clock you found in the attic fetched a few hundred pounds at auction. The porcelain figurine and the Art Deco lamp discovered at a boot fair were worth far in excess of what you paid for them. The set of Victorian-Chippendale chairs now gracing your dining room are worth over 10 times what you gave the previous owner, who had advertised them in the local newspaper but not realised their real value. The occasional stall you've taken at the antiques fair held half-a-dozen times a year in the village hall has made you a tidy profit on your initial outlay – all those weekend trips to jumble sales and junk shops have proved well worthwhile. What began as a hobby seems to be taking up more and more of your spare time. In fact, it's more interesting than your current job and, so far as you can see, potentially more lucrative if you worked at it full-time. Indeed, you've reached the point where you're thinking: why don't I start up my own antiques business.

My advice to anyone in this situation is: don't give up your day job before thinking through all the of the implications of buying and selling antiques full-time. Every year thousands of small businesses go into liquidation. While the reasons for this are many and varied, among the most common are underestimating what is involved, over-borrowing, cash-flow problems, and not setting up the business on a proper footing.

In previous chapters I have stressed the importance of becoming knowledgeable about antiques if you are to make money out of them, as well as what and what not to buy and the best ways of buying and selling to maximise your profit and minimise the risk of making a loss. All these acquired skills can, however, come to nothing if you ignore certain basic principles for setting up and running a business. If you are serious about this, here is some advice to help get you started on your own venture.

Seek advice from the experts

The Department of Trade and Industry sponsors various schemes to assist people thinking of setting up their own business. For example, the Small Business Advisory Service (local branches are listed in the telephone directory) offers free advice on the subject, can help you with drawing up a business plan – which will be of great assistance if you intend to approach your bank for a loan – and, under certain circumstances, can arrange government grants or subsidies to help get you off to a good start.

Securing a loan

You may be lucky enough to have acquired or made sufficient capital to build up your initial stock without having to borrow money. Servicing a debt while you are starting up a business (or at any time) is never particularly enjoyable. However, it may be unavoidable. If this is the case, the cheapest source of borrowing will be a loan or an authorised overdraft from your bank. The old-fashioned advice: cultivate your local bank manager, remains sound. Moreover, a reaction to the impersonal, computerised banking of the past decade or so seems to be gathering pace: banks make money by lending to their customers, and they are coming to realise, once again, that whether a particular customer is a good or bad risk is best judged by not only looking at a balance sheet, but also by the manager's personal assessment of the applicant. So, in addition to presenting your branch manager with a plausible business plan (many banks now have their own forms for this, and will often assist you with filling them in), it is also important to appear enthusiastic, knowledgeable, realistic, business-like and plausible. If you are able to secure a loan, it should go without saying that keeping up regular repayments, as well as telling your bank manager immediately if you start to get into difficulties, is vital. It's all too easy to let problems accumulate and stick your head in the sand. By talking to your manager, you may well discover the problems you thought were insurmountable can be overcome – repayments can be rescheduled, interest can be frozen etc.

Registering your business

If you trade under any name other than your own, or if you have a partner and aren't trading under both your names, you are bound by law to register the name of the business wit Companies House within 14 days of commencement of trading. (A law that also applies to married women who are trading under their maiden name.)

Employing an accountant

No one should start trading in the belief that can avoid the tax man or National Insurance contributions. Consequently, my advice is, comply with the law from the outset, employ an accountant and keep the tax man up-to-date.

A good accountant will save his fee many times over, chiefly by ensuring you don't make unnecessary payments and claiming your full entitlement to tax relief. Tax concessions change from year to year and an accountant will enable you to take full advantage of them. Your accountant can also liaise with the Department of Health and Social Security to sort out the National Insurance payments that you will be liable for under Schedule D as a self-employed person. An accountant will also be able to set-up a payroll if, in time, you expand and are able to take on some additional staf, either full- or part-time. For an accountant to work most efficiently (and economically) on your behalf there are various things that you can do to help:

1. Keep an up-to-date stock book, and enter every item you buy, including items you already owned when you started), giving each one a reference number and recording the date of purchase and, where relevant, the price paid. You should also record the date of sale for each item, together with the price it sold for – and keep the price tag from the item, which should display the reference number plus a brief description.

Not only will the stock book make it easier and quicker for an accountant to compile your end-of-year accounts, and/or quarterly V.A.T. returns (see below), it will also enable you to tell at a quick glance which items are selling quickly and which are proving difficult to shift.

2. Open a separate bank account for your business. Your accountant could do without having to sort out complications over what is business income and expenditure and personal money. In addition, ask the bank for a monthly statement, which will allow you to assess your cash flow, together with cheque and paying-in books with counterfoils, so that you can record details of each transaction. (Because of ever-increasing bank charges, you should also try to keep sufficient funds in your current account to obtain free banking.)

3. Keep an up-to-date notebook recording 'out-of-pocket' expenses, such as telephone calls and cab fares, together with receipts. Ideally, you should pay by cheque whenever possible, but sometimes the sums don't warrant this, and at other times a cash purchase may be demanded by the seller. It is worth keeping a notebook to record transactions at antique fairs and to transfer the information to a stock book at the end of the day.

V.A.T.

Value Added Tax is a serious matter: it comes under the aegis of Customs and Excise and, if you are liable and avoid payment, you could go to prison. Your accountant will able to tell you your income reaches the point where you become liable for V.A.T. (the threshold changes from year to year in the Chancellor's Budget).

So far as the antiques trade is concerned, Customs and Excise have two separate VAT schemes in operation at time of writing. The first involves the compulsory addition of VAT on the selling price of each item. The second, an optional scheme, involves VAT levied only on the difference between the purchase price and the selling price of an item – in other words, the gross profit. For obvious reasons, many dealers consider the Antiques Special Scheme is worth taking up, even though it involves keeping a 13-column ledger and recording the identity of both the customer you sold the item to, plus the person (or company) from whom you bought it. In addition, if you are liable for V.A.T. you will have to invoice all sales.

Given the work involved – you are, in effect, becoming an unpaid tax collector and have to complete a fair amount of complicated paperwork – some dealers deliberately restrict their trading so that they don't trip over the V.A.T. threshold. The disadvantage of this, however, is that when they buy anything from a V.A.T.-registered source they can not reclaim the V.A.T. percentage of the purchase price. Whether or not you limit the size of your business to avoid V.A.T. is up to you. Indeed, many antique dealers feel that they can make a perfectly satisfactory living under the V.A.T. threshold. However, deliberately restricting growth (and potentially greater profits) for this reason seems to me to be a rather short-sighted approach. Moreover, a good accountant can process virtually all of the tedious paperwork for you.

Postage

Once your business takes off you may well have to send items by post to clients in other parts of the country, or even abroad. While the vast majority of people are honest, there are one or two unscrupulous characters around. Consequently, I strongly recommend that you state your terms of business to all clients up-front: namely, on a payment with order basis – either cash, or if by cheque it must be cleared into your bank account before goods are despatched. You should also make a full refund on the return of goods if the customer is not satisfied.

When sending items by post, it is very important to pack them properly – double cartons, bubble wrapping etc. – to ensure their safe arrival. Registered packages, or those delivered by private courier, should also be insured against breakage in transit. (This isn't as expensive as you may think.)

Insurance

It is also important to insure your stock in situ – in other words, at home or in any other premises or outlets, such as a shop or market stall, that you are trading from. Insurance companies offer All Risks policies that cover fire, theft, accidental loss and damage. Cover can be extended to anywhere in the United Kingdom. With these policies, the value of a collection or any particular piece means its replacement value. If you make significant additions to your stock you should immediately inform the insurance company, who will then adjust the cover.and increase you premium.

Suing for debt

In addition to covering yourself against non-payment for items despatched by post, you should also avoid risks when making face-to-face transactions. Antique dealing, is largely a cash trade, even nowadays. Consequently, you should establish a cash-on-the-nail rule, and stick to it. Avoid giving credit, even to people you know well. However, if something should go wrong, seek redress via the Small Claims Court. (Information on this is available from both your local Citizens Advice Bureau and the County Court.)

It is important to note that if you win such a case you can apply for payment of the expenses you incur in proceeding with the claim. If you lose, however, you will be liable to pay the other side's court fees, travelling expenses and loss of earnings incurred during their appearance in the court.

You may also like to take some comfort from the fact that precedent says most non-payers pay up when threatened with a summons. This is probably largely explained by the fact that cases involving debt are scrutinised by all the major credit agencies, and the subsequent bad credit rating will adversely affect any future applications for credit.

Transport

Buying and selling antiques on any scale will almost certainly involve a fair amount of travelling. Therefore, you will need either an estate car or a van, depending on the sort of antiques you are dealing in. Your accountant will be able to advise you on the merits of having either a company car or a privately owned one and charge the mileage on to the company.

The tax concessions on this are forever changing, as are the AA (Automobile Association) approved mileage rates for particular types of vehicle, and the option you choose will depend partly on how many miles you cover per annum.

It is also important to have specific car insurance that will cover business use and theft as well. Check this out with your insurance company, but shop around as rates vary quite considerably between different insurance companies and you don't want to pay over the odds..

Trading from home

My advice to anyone who is just starting to trade in antiques is don't rush into renting a shop. This is a major financial commitment that involves signing a lease for a period of years (usually between one and five years these days), and paying for costly shop fittings and decorations. Moreover, premium locations are understandably expensive, particularly in large cities, while back-street premises, although cheaper, inevitably attract far fewer customers.

Consequently, when starting out there is a very strong case for combining trading from home with renting stalls in antique markets and at antique fairs. However, when conducting your own business from your home you must be careful not to infringe Planning Regulations. The Town and Country Planning Act stipulates that if there is any material change in the use of a building, planning permission is required, and problems arise because each local authority tends to interpret 'material change' in a different way.

The plain fact of the matter is, most antique dealers starting up a business overcome this potential problem by keeping their heads down. In other words, they don't turn a large part of the house over to the storage and sale of antiques, and they don't put up advertising signs, use their front windows for display or have hordes of customers or delivery vans coming and going. However, once a business has expanded to the point where this is unavoidable, then commercial premises, such as a shop or regular stall must be taken on.

Advertising

I have already mentioned, in Chapter Six, the importance of advertising if you are selling antiques. However, from a purely business point of view, you should note that it is very easy to waste money in this area. An American tycoon once said that his companies were spending twice as much money on advertising as they needed, and the only factor that was stopping him from cutting the budget for this in half was that he didn't know which half to cut.

My advice to anyone starting up an antiques business and advertising on a limited budget is that, while personal contact is very important, the printed word tends to be more durable, provided you get it right. More specifically, while cheap and poorly designed letter headings and trade cards often leave the potential client feeling uneasy – can they trust you? – a smart and well-presented introduction always makes a favourable impression and tempts the reader to make further contact. Consequently, it is well worth using a good commercial artist to produce letter headings and trade cards. The additional costs will invariably pay for themselves in the long run.

In addition, you should place an entry in a reputable trade directory, such as Yellow Pages, and advertise consistently – not on a one-off basis – in the classified columns of local newspapers and, if you specialise in a particular field, trade journals. (Many papers and periodicals offer reduced rates for a long-term booking of, say, three to six months.) Having done this, you should carefully monitor the response to the ads by asking callers where they heard about you. If you get a poor response, don't renew.

Trade Descriptions Act

In common with all other business activities, the buying and selling of antiques comes under the Trades Description Act. Consequently, if you offer a description of something, or are asked for a certificate of authenticity, and it turns about to be something other than what you said it was, you could be sued. Obviously passing off something like E.P.N.S. (Electro-Plated Nickel Silver) as Sheffield Plate would be plain stupid and downright dishonest. However, because there is considerable ambiguity over the provenance and authenticity of many antiques, particularly certain items of furniture, the simple rule is: if you are not absolutely sure what something is, say so – there is a considerable legal difference between describing something as 'Georgian' and 'probably Georgian'.

Joining Associations

If you decide to trade in antiques full-time, you should consider joining one of the two leading antique dealer associations in Britain: B.A.D.A. (the British Antique Dealer Association) and L.A.P.A.D.A. (the Association of Art and Antique Dealers). Addresses for both organisations are listed at the back of the book. The chief advantages of membership is the confidence it instils in potential customers, regarding your knowledge of antiques and your professional integrity. It is also an exmtremely useful way to establish yourself amongst your fellow dealers and to network at various gatherings and fairs organised by the associations..

B.A.D.A.

Becoming a member of B.A.D.A. (the British Antique Dealer Association) is not simply a matter of sending off an application form and an annual subscription. It is a relatively small and exclusive body, with membership that rarely exceeds 500. To be considered for membership, you must have been trading in your own right for a minimum of three years (almost invariably from your own premises).

Having fulfilled that criteria, you must find two existing members, who are willing to propose and second you for membership, you will then be 'vetted' to see if you are reputable. This will include an unannounced visit to your premises and/or a stand at an antiques fair, to see if all items on display are properly labelled with accurate descriptions etc. If you pass all these tests with flying colours, you may well be elected to membership. (At the time of writing, the annual subscription is £500.) However, you should note that many proposed memberships are turned down, and others are deferred to some time in the future (in other words, you are, in effect, put on a waiting list).

You should also note that membership is reviewed annually – in other words, the organisation is, quite rightly, strict regarding professional conduct, and any departure from their high standards is unacceptable.

If elected, you will be able to put B.A.D.A. on letter heads and any other correspondence. You will also be able to display the B.A.D.A. logo in and outside your premises. The organisation will also keep you posted on forthcoming antique fairs and auctions etc., and provide help with legal problems.

L.A.P.A.D.A.

This is a slightly larger organisation, with some 750 members at the time of writing. To be eligible for membership, applicants must have been trading in antiques and have been registered for at least three years.

They must also be able to demonstrate 'knowledge and integrity in their chosen field', provide two referees (preferably L.A.P.A.D.A. members), who have known them for a minimum of five years or have been in business for at least 10 years, and allow their premises/stock to be vetted and/or their stand at trade fairs to be inspected.

If elected to membership, there is a one-off joining fee of, at the time of writing, £100 (which is waived if you are already a member of a recognised art and antiques association). The annual subscription is, at present, £268. As with B.A.D.A., the Association of Art and Antique Dealers, strictly enforce their own Code of Practice, and membership will be reviewed if any transgression occurs.

Finally, if some of the above sounds rather daunting I hope it won't put you off setting up an antiques business. If you stick to the few simple rules mentioned in this book you will find there's good money to be made - after all, when was the last time you saw an antiques dealer travelling to work on a bike.

GLOSSARY OF TRADESPEAK

When you become involved with buying and selling antiques, and especially as you begin to barter with other dealers, you are likely to encounter various turns of phrase exclusive to the trade. Knowing what they mean, and being able to use them yourself, conveys the impression you know what you're talking about and helps to confirm you as a fellow professional. As a result, you are far more likely to be able to buy for a better price than if you appeared to be an innocent abroad (i.e. a member of the public). A word of warning, however, some of the slang listed below can best be described as 'barrow-boy' language, and while it is entirely appropriate when, for example, talking to runners or traders at Bermondsey market; it won't go down very well in Harrogate or Bond Street.

'*AF*' meaning 'As Found': A term that often appears in auction catalogues and denotes that the piece in question is badly damaged or in poor condition.

A steal: An item bought for well under its true market value, or a piece offered for sale at a supposedly cheap price.

Bent: Either means the piece has been stolen or that there is something not quite right about it – i.e. it has been 'doctored' in some way.

Brassed up: Refers to a piece of furniture that has had brass handles substituted for the original wooden ones, and possibly other brass embellishments, such as stringing, added to enhance the attractiveness of the piece to potential buyers who like that sort of thing.

Clean: A piece that has no flaws. However, be careful, as in practice this sometimes means only visible ones.

Collector's piece: Occasionally used to describe an item that is highly collectable, but more usually refers to a piece that is so weird only an eccentric collector would be interested in it.

Come right: Refers to a piece that a dealer has paid too much for, but implies that it will become a good investment.

Cut: Usually refers to a piece of furniture that has been cut down to make it smaller and therefore more saleable and valuable. There's an old saying in the trade: 'every inch under 3 foot is worth another £100'.

Decorator's piece: Usually a disparaging term used to describe a piece that has little intrinsic value or artistic merit, but is currently fashionable among interior decorators and designers who may well be prepared to pay over-the-odds for it knowing they can, in turn, charge one of their clients a hefty sum.

Distressing: Also known as antiquing, this is the process of artificially ageing a piece by simulating the natural wear and tear you would expect to have accumulated over the years. Extreme examples include bashing a reproduction oak refectory table with a motorcycle chain to create dents.

Doesn't leave much: A dealer's response when told the price of something by another dealer and implying that it is too high and, therefore, would not enable him or her to make a worthwhile profit on a subsequent sale of said item.

Gear: A sundry collection of pieces for sale – bent gear means that they have been stolen.

Honest: Refers to a totally genuine if unpretentious piece, but be wary if it is used – coming from the unscrupulous it can mean exactly the opposite.

Insider dealing: The buying and selling of antiques within the trade – dealer to dealer. See page 14.

Jockey: An advisor or courier employed by a foreign buyer to accompany him or her on buying trips around antiques shops.

Kitsch: Over-decorated and vulgar pieces that appeal to popular bad taste; always a derogatory term.

Knocker: A travelling dealer who knocks on doors unsolicited and tries to talk unsuspecting owners into selling pieces in their home for substantially less than their true worth. Very prevalent in the 1960s and '70s, they are now, fortunately, a dying breed mainly due to bad publicity and a greater awareness among the general public of the value of antiques.

Knockout: see Ring.

Kosher: A totally genuine piece that looks and is right.

Lump: A particularly large and heavy piece of furniture that is difficult to move.

Marriage: The joining together of two unrelated pieces (mainly furniture) to make a more saleable and valuable piece — such as a bookcase on top of a bureau to make a bureau-bookcase.

More lead than silver: A disparaging observation used to describe an item of silverware (such as a teapot) that has been substantially or often repaired.

No trade left in it: Refers to a piece that has changed hands among dealers to such an extent that the only way to get rid of it now (and make a profit) is to sell to a retail customer.

Off the wall: An auctioneers technique, which is perfectly legal, for taking fictitious bids from the wall in order to raise the bidding to the level of the vendor's reserve. In the 'rooms' (the leading London auction houses) this is also known as 'off the chandelier'.

Period: An item that was made when it was supposed to have been made, and has all the styling and attributes you would expect of a piece made during said period. However, there is often a question mark attached: 'is it period?' means 'is it what it appears, or later?'.

Punter: A potential customer (invariably a member of the general public or a collector).

Ring: For a detailed explanation, see pages 104-105.

Running up: A practice that occasionally occurs at auctions when a dealer (or sometimes more than one) will deliberately bid or run up the price of a piece in order to discourage a new dealer or a member of the public from bidding for another piece or even coming back to another auction. Some auctioneers have also been known to do this to speed up the pace of bidding and thereby trip the unsuspecting into bidding more than they might have originally intended to.

Smalls: Refers to any small piece, other than pictures, carpets and rugs or furniture.

Tarted up: Refers to any piece, but usually an item of furniture, that has been superficially restored and polished to make it more saleable and valuable.

Turn it up: A turn of phrase used by dealers when they ask another dealer if they can inspect the underneath and/or back of a piece of furniture.

Turns up well: Although occasionally used to refer to a genuine piece, usually a cynical turn of phrase used to denote that a faker has paid as much attention to the underside as the top of a piece — knowing that the former is precisely where anyone will look to check if the item is authentic.

What's the best you can do? The first question a dealer asks another dealer when interested in buying a piece and keen to haggle over the price.

Zipping up: The opposite of distressing, this is the process of making a piece more exotic. Examples include insetting marquetry applying layers of varnish and polish to accentuate (or to create) a patina.

FURTHER READING

£

Miller's Titles

Miller's Antiques Price Guide
Miller's Collectables Price Guide
(The above two titles are published
annually with completely new entries
every year)
Antiques & Collectables – The
    Facts at Your Fingertips
Understanding Antiques
Antiques Encyclopedia
Care & Repair of Antiques
    & Collectables
Antiques Shops, Fairs & Auctions 2000

Miller's Buyers Guides

Art Nouveau & Art Deco
Ceramics
Chinese & Japanese Antiques
Clocks & Barometers
Late Georgian to Edwardian Furniture
Pine & Country Furniture

Miller's Antiques Checklists

Art Deco
Art Nouveau
Clocks
Furniture
Glass
Jewellery
Porcelain
Pottery
Silver & Plate
Toys & Games
Victorian

General

Museums and Galleries in Great
    Britain and Ireland
    British Leisure Publications
    (pub. annually)

Guide to Town and Country Auctions in
    Britain. Eric Green.
    A.A. Publications (1994)
The Museums Yearbook
    The Museums Association
    (pub. annually)
The Penguin Dictionary of
Decorative Arts.
    John Fleming and Hugh Honour.
    Viking (1989)
The Illustrated History of Antiques.
Huon Mallalieu.
    Aurum Press (1993)

Clocks

Watchmakers and Clockmakers of the
World (volume 1). G.H. Baillie.
    NAG Press (1974)
Watchmakers and Clockmakers of the
World (volume 2). Brian Loomes.
    NAG Press (1976)

Furniture

Discovering English Furniture. John Bly.
    Shire (1976)
The Antiques Directory.
Furniture. J&M Miller.
    Mitchell Beazley (1985)
The Dictionary of English Furniture.
Ralph Edwards.
    Country Life (1953)
Fine Points of Furniture. Albert Sack.
    Crown (New York)(1950)
World Furniture. Helena Hayward.
    Hamlyn (1965)

Glass

An Illustrated Dictionary of Glass.
Harold Newman.
    Thames and Hudson (1977)

English Drinking Glasses.
  L.M. Bickerton.
  Barrie and Jenkins (1971)

Metal Wares

The Collectors Dictionary of the
Silver and Gold of Great
Britain and South America.
  Michael Clayton
  Antique Collectors Club (1985)
An Illustrated History of English Plate.
Sir Charles James Jackson.
  Macmillan (1905)
American Silversmiths and Their Marks.
Stephen Ensko.
  Ensko (New York) (1975)
Encyclopedia of American
Silver Manufacturers.
  Dorothy T. Rainwater.
  Crown (New York) (1975)
Pewter of the Western World.
  P.R.G. Hornsby.
  *Shiffer, Exton PA and
  Moorland (1983)*
Collecting Copper and Brass.
  Geoffrey Wills.
  Mayflower (1970)
Antique Sheffield Plate. G.B. Hughes.
  Batsford (1970)

Pottery and Porcelain

The History of Porcelain. Paul Atterbury.
  Orbis (1982)
British Porcelain. Geoffrey Godden.
Barrie and Jenkins (1974)
British Pottery. Geoffrey Godden.
  Barrie and Jenkins (1974)

USEFUL ADDRESSES

B.A.D.A.
The British Antique
Dealers' Association
20 Rutland Gate,
London SW7 1BD

L.A.P.A.D.A.
The Association of Art and
Antique Dealers
535 Kings Road,
London SW10 0SZ

**The Society of London
Art Dealers**
91 Jermyn Street,
London SW1Y 6JB

The Antique Collectors' Club
5 Church Street,
Woodbridge,
Suffolk IP12 1DS

Christie's
8 King Street
St. James's
London SW1Y 6QT

Christie's South Kensington
85 Old Brompton Road
London SW7 3LD

Sotheby's
34-35 New Bond Street
London W1A 2AD

Phillips
101 New Bond Street
London W1Y OAS

Bonham's
Montpelier Galleries
Montpelier Street
London SW7 1AP

MILLER'S CLUB

Miller's produce a regular newsletter with articles on antiques and
collecting, as well as information on new books. If you would like a
FREE copy, please write to us at: Miller's Club,
2-4 Heron Quays, Docklands, London E14 4JP

HOW TO MAKE MONEY
OUT OF ANTIQUES

——————— £ ———————

ANTIQUES INVENTORY

Description of the piece (including size, materials and decorative features)	Details about the piece's condition

Documenting your collection is an essential discipline. Whether you intend to sell items on and need to assess your profit or plan to keep them and need information for insurance purposes, you will find an inventory a useful source of reference.

The tables below show the information you should record. Why not use these pages to jot down notes while you're out and about or photocopy them to use in your own files at home?

Note: Keep the receipts of anything you purchase with the inventory, plus photographs if possible.

Information about the piece's history	Place of purchase	Date of purchase	Price paid

Description of the piece (including size, materials and decorative features)	Details about the piece's condition

Information about the piece's history	Place of purchase	Date of purchase	Price paid

INDEX

abrasions, on furniture 119
accountants 152-3
Act of Parliament clocks 79
advertising 93-4, 4, 139, 157-8
alcohol stains 128
alterations, furniture 36-7
amber, cleaning 125
antique fairs 30-1, 108, 139, 140-5, 157
antiques trade 14-25
aquamarine, cleaning 125
armchairs 47-8, 111-12
arms and armour 84-6
Art Deco 82
Art Nouveau 77, 82
Association of Art and Antique Dealers (L.A.P.A.D.A.) 32, 105, 108, 159, 160-1
associations 159-60
attics 88
auction catalogues 28, 29-30, 100, 136
auction rings 104-5, 135
auctions 21-2, 29-30, 94-105, 109, 135-7
automata 87

badges 85
Ball, William 62
bank accounts 153
bank loans 151-2
barometers 80
Baxter, T. 69
beds 44
beer stains 128
beeswax 121
beetroot stains 128
bidding, auctions 102-4
Bierce, Ambrose 105
Billingsley, William 67, 69
bleaching, on furniture 114
blood stains 128
bloom, removing 114
bone china 56
bookcases 44-5
books 26-7
boot fairs 22, 92-3, 108, 138
Boreman, Zachariah 61
Bittger, J.F. 64
Bow polychrome 56
Bow 56, 60, 61, 67
brass, cleaning 116, 122
brass fittings 38-9
breakfront bookcases 44
Brewer, John 61
Bristol porcelain 57, 61, 70
Britannia metal 77

British Antique Dealers Association (B.A.D.A.) 16, 32, 105, 108, 159-60
British Antique Furniture Restorer's Association (B.A.F.R.A.) 113
bronze 82, 123
bruises, removing 114-15
bureau-bookcases 44
bureaux 45
business plans 151, 152
buying antiques 88-109

cabinets 45-6
cameos, cleaning 125-6
candle wax, removing 115, 129
canework, repairs 119
Canterburies 46
car boot sales 22, 92-3, 108, 138
card tables 53
carpets 82-4
carriage, costs 135-6
carriage clocks 80
carving, on furniture 39
catalogues 28, 29-30, 100, 136
Caughley 57, 58, 59, 70

172

cleaning 121-2
ceramics 55-71
Cescinsky, Herbert 34
Chaffers, Richard &
    Partners 61-2
chairs 47-8
chandeliers,
    cleaning 124
Chantilly 58
charity shops 22, 89,
    91
Chelsea porcelain
    58-9, 60
cheques 143, 155
chests 48-9, 52
chiffoniers 46
Chinese porcelain 71
chocolate stains 129
Christian, Philip 62
chrome, cleaning 123
cleaning 110, 113-14
    ceramics 121-2
    furniture 114-19
    glass 124-5
    jewelry 125-7
    metals 122-4
    textiles 128-31
clocks 78-80
clothes presses 49
clubs 139
Coalport 59-60, 65,
    67, 69
coffee stains 129
coffers 48
Colt revolvers 86
commission 101, 135,
    136, 137
commodes 47
Companies
    House 152
continental silver
    marks 73
copies, furniture 37-8
copper, cleaning 123

coral, cleaning 126
corner cupboards 49
court cupboards 49
cradles 44
cupboards 49
Customs and
    Excise 154

Davenport
    porcelain 60
Davenports 50
dealers 14-24, 31-2,
    105-9
debt, suing for 155-6
dents, removing
    114-15
Department of Health
    and Social Security
    152-3
Department of Trade
    and Industry 151
Derby porcelain 60-1,
    66, 67
desks 49-51
dial clocks 80
diamanté, cleaning 126
diamonds, cleaning
    126
dining chairs 48
discounts 108, 137
displays 134,
    141, 146
dolls 87
dovetail joints 41
drawers 40-2, 48-9
dressers 49
drinks trays 53
drop-leaf tables 53
dumb waiters 51
Duvivier 66

earthenware 61
edged weapons 85
electro-plate 76

emeralds, cleaning 126
enamelled glass,
    cleaning 124
engraved glass,
    cleaning 125
estimates, auctions
    30, 100
expenses 153

fairs 139, 140-5
fakes 26, 30, 34-5,
    38-9, 108
fat stains 129
finances:
    accountants 152-3
    bank loans 151-2
    cheques 155
firearms 85-6
flintlocks 85-6
fly marks 115
forgeries 34-5, 108
four poster beds 44
frames, mirrors 52
French polish 38, 120
friends, buying and
    selling from 89,
    137-8
fruit juice stains 129
furniture:
    cleaning 114-19
    minor repairs
    119-21
    re-upholstering
    111-12
    reviving and
    polishing 121
    what to look for
    36-54

gate-leg tables 53
Gilbody, Samuel 61
glass 81, 82
    cleaning 124-5
    mirrors 52

grease stains 116
grime, removing 115-16

hallmarks, silver 72-3, 74
handles, drawers 42
hard paste porcelain 55
Herold, C.F. 65
Herold, J.G. 64, 65
Hill, Jockey 61
hinges 43
holes, furniture repairs 120
home, trading from 18, 138-40, 157

ink stains 116, 129
inlays, cleaning 117
insurance 155, 156
international fairs 144-5
iron, cleaning 116, 123
iron mould stains 129-30
ivory 82, 126

jade, cleaning 126
jet, cleaning 127
jewelry, cleaning 125-7
joints, dovetail 41
jumble sales 22, 89-91, 108
junk shops 22, 91-2, 138

Kändler, J.J. 65
Kayser, Engelbert 77
Klinger, J.G. 65
kneehole desks 49-50

Lalique, René 81
lantern clocks 79
lead, cleaning 123
lead glass 81
learning about antiques 26-33
Liberty 77
Littler, William 63
Liverpool wares 61-3
loans, banks 151-2
local fairs 140-3
long case clocks 79
Longton Hall 63, 66
lowboys 53
Lowestoft porcelain 63-4

magazines 27-8
mark-ups 133
markets 20-1, 30-1, 108, 146-7, 157
marks: pewter 76-7
porcelain and pottery 55-6
Sheffield Plate 76
silver 72-3, 74
marquetry 43
marriages 37, 49, 50, 51, 75, 78, 84
Meissen 58, 60-1, 64-5, 68, 69
Mennecy 70
metal wares 72-7
metals, cleaning 116, 122-4
mildew stains 130
militaria 85
milk stains 130
Minton 60, 65-6, 67
mirrors 52, 125
mother-of-pearl, cleaning 117
museums 29

nail varnish stains 130
national fairs 144-5
National Insurance 152-3
Newhall 65, 66
Niedermayer, J.J. 69

oak furniture 51-2
occasional tables 53-
'off the wall', bidding at auctions 103-4
oil stains 116, 129
opals, cleaning 127
Oriental porcelain 71
ormolu, cleaning 117

paint, removing 117-18, 130
parquetry, cleaning 118
pastiches, furniture 39
patination 40, 74, 110
pearls, cleaning 127
pedestal desks 50-1
Pegg, 'Quaker' 61
Pennington, James, John and Seth 62
periodicals 27-8
pewter 76-7, 123-4
Pinxton 65, 66-7
pistols 85-6
planning permission 157
Plymouth porcelain 67
Podmore, Robert 61
polish, French 38, 120
polishing furniture 121
porcelain 55-71
cleaning 121-2
pottery 55-6
cleaning 121-2

powder flasks **85**

prices **132-3**
  auction catalogues
  30, 100
  price guides **28-9**
  and profits **148-9**

private treaty
  sales **104**

provincial fairs **143-4**

refectory tables **53**

registering
  businesses **152**

Reid, William **62**

Reinicke, Paul **65**

repairs **26, 34-5, 36,
  110-11, 113, 119-21**

reproductions **26, 38**

reserves, auction
  prices **104,
  135, 136**

restoration **26, 35,
  36-7, 107,
  110-14**

revolvers **86**

rings, auction
  104-5, 135

Rockingham **60, 65,
  67**

Roman glass **81**

rubies, cleaning **12**

rugs **82-4**

'runners' **21, 106,
  107, 147-8**

rust **116, 123**

St Cloud **68, 70**

sale previews
  29-30, 100

Samson Edmie
  et Cie **68**

sapphires,
  cleaning **127**

scorch marks **131**

scratches, on
  furniture **119, 120**

selling antiques **132-49**

setting up in business
  150-61

Sèvres **59-60, 68-9**

Sheffield Plate
  75-6, 124

shoe polish stains **131**

shops **16, 17-18, 20,
  22, 30-1, 89, 91-2,
  138, 145-6, 157**

side tables **53**

sideboards **45-6**

silver **72-6, 124**

skeleton clocks **80**

Small Business
  Advisory Service **151**

Small Claims Court
  156

soapstone porcelain
  57, 59

societies **139**

sofa tables **54**

sofas **111-12**

soft paste
  porcelain **55**

Soqui, Monsieur **67**

Spode **65**

stained glass,
  cleaning **125**

stately homes **29**

steel, rust **116**

Steiff **87**

Steuben **82**

Swansea porcelain **69**

swords **85**

tables **52, 53-4**

tallboys **36**

tar stains **118**

taxation **152**
  V.A.T. **101, 109,
  135, 136, 153, 154**

teddy bears **87, 100**

textiles, cleaning
  128-31

Tiffany & Co. **81,
  82, 88**

tortoiseshell,
  cleaning **127**

toys **87**

Trades Descriptions
  Act **108-9, 158-9**

transport **156**

Tunbridgeware **106-7**

turquoise,
  cleaning **127**

United Kingdom
  Institute for
  Conservation **113**

upholstery **48, 53,
  111-12**

V.A.T. **101, 109, 135,
  136, 153, 154**

veneers **42-3**

Vienna porcelain **69**

Vincennes **58, 70**

wall clocks **79**

walnut furniture **54**

wardrobes **49**

washing china **122**

water marks **118-19**

wax: polishing
  furniture **121**
  removing **115,
  117, 129**

weapons **85-6**

wine coolers **54**

Wolfe & Co **62-3**

woodworm **120-1**

Worcester porcelain
  57, 67, 70-1